SUMMER OF LIGHT

Summer
of
Light

Dennis M. Van Wey

CROSSWAY BOOKS • WESTCHESTER, ILLINOIS
A DIVISION OF GOOD NEWS PUBLISHERS

*To my wife Pat
for sharing a dream
and helping to
make it come true*

IOWA

*I*t was Summer 1961 in McKinley, Iowa. We were a family of four living close to the Mississippi River and closer to poverty. It could have been worse. Dad always said there were millions of people in Asia who would have thought the Kane family lived like kings. He was usually drunk when he said it.

On a sweltering Saturday late in July, I was lying in our porch swing sipping a root beer whose fizz had dwindled in much the same manner as my initiative. From a nearby tree a songbird called to its mate. I closed my eyes and listened to the melodic chirpings of love. The air was so warm and peaceful. Suddenly the bird seemed to whistle my name: "Tom Kane. Tom Tom Kane."

"Huh?"

I sat up and saw Jimmy Swailes running across the street toward me, dribbling a beautiful, new, brown-orange basketball. Jimmy and I were best friends, although neither of us would have admitted it. Such things were assumed, but never verbalized.

"Tom! Hey, Tommygun, look what I got!"

The grin on his face was wide enough to hold a potted plant. He didn't look like a kid whose father had shipped him to church camp for a week just to placate a wealthy, religious aunt.

"Let's see it," I yelled.

He threw the ball to me, and I caressed the virgin leather. There was something wonderful about the feel of a new piece of athletic equipment, especially to kids who had once been forced to play football with a cantaloupe rind.

"It's fabulous," I said. "Where did you get it?"

"I won it at camp for knowing the most Bible verses."

"Bible verses?"

"Yep."

"Since when do you know anything about the Bible?"

"I just started learning this past week. They taught us a lot of neat stuff. Gimme the ball and I'll show you something." Jimmy put the ball on the end of his finger and gave it several slaps with his other hand. The more he slapped the side of the ball, the faster it spun. When he pulled the other hand away, the ball rotated perfectly atop his slender finger like a gyroscope.

"Let me try that," I said.

I attempted to duplicate his effort while he talked about his week at camp.

"We had it made, Tommy. We went swimming twice a day in this big lake, and we played ball all the time, and once we even got to take canoes out on the river. I wish you coulda been there."

I was having a great deal of difficulty balancing the ball for more than half a second. This proved irritating, but not nearly so much as the discovery that Jimmy had been having a good time the past week instead of suffering as I had believed.

"I got better things to do than hang out at some wimpy Bible camp," I said.

"You would have liked it," he insisted.

"Don't tell me what I would have liked, you redheaded jerk."

Splotches of pink colored Jimmy's freckle-speckled face. Sunlight glinted off his glasses. I waited for my insult to unleash the famous Swailes temper. Instead, he swallowed and gave a weak grin.

"You can't make me mad anymore, Tommy. I'm different now."

Who was he kidding? Anybody could make Jimmy Swailes mad anytime anywhere. He was the head of a match, needing only the slightest bit of friction to ignite. He was an explosion awaiting detonation. Making Jimmy mad was one of my favorite pastimes, and today was no exception—especially since I couldn't do his dumb ball trick.

"You're different all right. Everybody at that camp was probably different. I bet they made you guys wear dresses and walk around with Bibles on your heads."

He shrugged. "It won't work, Tommy. I've really changed."

There was a pause as he waited for me to say something and I waited for him to start laughing, or tell me he was just being cute. A certain look in his eyes told me it would be a long wait. That really made me mad.

"You must have got hit in the head with a bat while you was at that camp. Your brains are scrambled."

"Guess I just see things a little different since Wednesday night."

"What's so hot about Wednesday night?"

Jimmy seemed to struggle for the right words. He finally took a deep breath and looked me in the eyes. "I found Jesus Christ."

"I didn't know he was lost."

Jimmy's ears reddened. "That's not what I meant. I was trying to say that I got myself saved."

"From who—Dracula?"

It was hard to know how to react to what he was saying. My friend seemed quite serious, but I felt like laughing. He was enthused, but I couldn't have cared less. On another day I might have responded more positively, but at that moment all I could do was shake my head in disgust and concentrate harder on balancing the basketball on my finger. I gave an extra-hard slap to make it rotate faster, but succeeded only in spinning it right out of my hand. The ball hit the sidewalk right between Jimmy and me, then bounced at a crazy angle into the street.

"I'll get it," Jimmy said, running to retrieve his prize before it reached the downhill grade and rolled for two city blocks.

It was then that my mother stepped onto the porch and yelled something about coming in for lunch. As I turned toward her, the air was suddenly filled with the ugly shriek of tires being ground against unyielding concrete. Mom's hand flew to her mouth; the color left her face like light leaves a switched-off bulb. Over my shoulder I saw a battered red pickup depart the street and begin plowing a neighbor's terrace with the front bumper. It came to rest against a badly-shaken pear tree, and unripe fruit rained upon the hood. The horn began to honk. People rushed to their porches and front lawns to see what had happened.

I started to run in the direction of the pickup with two questions in my head: did I know the driver, and was it possible to eat some of those green pears? Those thoughts faded when I saw Jimmy Swailes in the street. He lay motionless except for one leg kicking weakly into the air, as if trying to ward off the invisible grasp of death. His face was torn and bloodied, and the hot pavement beneath his head was slowly being covered with an oozing red. Several feet away, his basketball rested against the curb. Something needed to be done, but I could only stand and stare at my friend as his life ebbed away from him. The last sound he ever made was a half-groan—half-gurgle that nobody heard but me. By the time Old Man Carver, our neighbor, knelt down beside Jimmy, the kicking had stopped. My friend's eyes were open toward the sky, but they saw nothing. Somebody covered his face with a dish-towel. Almost immediately a dark stain showed through.

An angry crowd gathered around the pickup. The door was jerked open, and a Mexican in jeans and a yellow shirt was pulled out. The honking stopped, and the sound of a distant siren took its place. Somebody punched the Mexican's face, but he barely seemed to notice as he fought loose and staggered in the direction of Jimmy's body. I watched him come to the edge of the grass and stumble into the street. A trickle of blood trailed from one nostril and down across his upper lip. His forehead was split open. Black hair glistened as it sat in thick waves atop his brown face. He was grinning.

"Get outta the street when I drive," he yelled at Jimmy.

"He's dead, you fool," said Old Man Carver, his voice trembling. The Mexican kept grinning. "Get outta the street when I drive!"

I wanted to hurt him. I wanted to put a fist into his crooked teeth and turn them into powder, but my arms were leaden. At the worst possible time, my body had betrayed me; my muscles refused to work.

A squad car slid around the corner a block away from us, siren wailing.

"Stinkin' cops," laughed the Mexican.

As two men in blue got out of the car, a woman came screaming from between the houses. Mrs. Swailes lost one of her shoes as she ran into the street calling her son's name. Old Man Carver tried to hold her back, but she brushed him aside. One of the police officers reached Jimmy the same time as the mother and squeezed a limp wrist in search of a pulse. Mrs. Swailes fell to her knees beside her son, still calling his name. She pulled the dishtowel off his face and screamed again. The creeping red stain was now on the hem of her dress.

"The ambulance is on the way," said the other officer as he watched his partner's fruitless search for a sign of life.

"Is he dead?" asked Mrs. Swailes.

"I'm afraid he might be," said the younger cop, the one holding Jimmy's wrist.

The older officer gave his partner a subtle nudge in the back with his knee. "We'll have to let a doctor decide that, ma'am. Let's just hope it works out."

"How did this happen?" the distraught mother asked the crowd forming around her.

The Mexican wiped away the blood from under his nose, and some of it smeared his cheek. "Get outta the street when I drive," he said shrugging, as if that one line explained everything.

The older cop stepped over to him. "You the driver of that pickup?"

"That's me, boy."

"You been drinkin'?"

The Mexican looked at a bump on his forearm that had started to discolor. He rubbed it. "I hurt my stinkin' arm."

The officer pulled out a set of handcuffs. "You just ran a kid into the street, so don't expect me to worry about your health. Turn around."

Another siren could be heard off toward town. Mrs. Swailes was no longer speaking to her son, only weeping and sniffling and swaying on her knees, as if she might topple at any second. The Mexican backed away from the cop, looking serious for the first time since the accident.

"I need to go to home," he said.

The policeman put a hand on his nightstick. His eyes were mean. "You stop right there or I'll crack your head like a coconut."

A couple of the men who had been standing over by the pickup now positioned themselves behind the Mexican. As he turned to run, they grabbed him and pulled him to the ground. "You ain't goin' nowhere, Jose," grunted one of them, shoving the Mexican's face into the grass.

The cop snapped open the cuffs. "Bend them arms behind his back."

"Get police," screamed the Mexican.

The other man, U.S.M.C. tattooed on his large bicep, drove a foot into the side of the Mexican's skull. I saw the dark eyes flicker momentarily, then grow large with fear. "Get outta the street when I drive!"

"Help me get him into the squad car," the officer told the men. An ambulance pulled alongside the police car as the Mexican was dragged toward it. Two attendants, one wearing white and one in plain clothes, jumped out and ran to where Jimmy lay. Between them they carried a large medical kit.

"Is he dead?" asked Mrs. Swailes before they even reached the body.

One attendant pulled a stethoscope from the kit and opened Jimmy's shirt to search for a heartbeat. The younger police officer stepped back out of the way as the other attendant shined a small light into Jimmy's eyes.

"No pupil reaction," said the attendant.

"I can't get a beat," said the other.

Mrs. Swailes collapsed to the pavement, beating her fist against it in choking rage.

The young cop walked back to the squad car and reached through an open window for the radio. He requested that the coroner be dispatched to the scene. His uniform shirt was sweat-darkened, and his hand appeared to tremble. Perhaps it was just the car shaking as the Mexican put up one last struggle by wrapping a leg around the doorpost while his captors tried to push him inside. The older cop finally drew out his nightstick and mashed it across the Mexican's shin. The troublesome leg pulled quickly inward, like a wounded spider's, and resisted no more.

The ambulance attendant put his stethoscope back into the medical kit. The young cop returned to Mrs. Swailes and tried to convince her to get out of the sun. The two men who helped subdue the Mexican brushed themselves off and muttered something about "wetbacks in this town." The older cop got into the back of the squad car with the Mexican, who was yelling Spanish obscenities at those outside. Old Man Carver remained beside Jimmy's body, brushing away the flies that had paused to sample spilt blood. A wrecker came down the street, and so did another police car.

Suddenly there was too much noise—sirens, blaring radios, everybody yelling orders. The sun became too hot. There was too much blood, too many people, not enough air. I had to get away. My wobbly legs were barely capable of propelling me to a spot behind our lilac bushes, where I threw up. Then Mom was there holding me to her chest and promising that everything was going to be all right. I wanted to believe her, but Jimmy lay dead in the street. Nothing could ever make that all right!

• • • •

Late that evening I was sitting in the porch swing staring out at the dark spot in the street. It was strange how something as vividly red as fresh blood could turn black after being exposed to sunlight and air. Maybe that was a good thing. While it had remained red, the spot out there was still a part of my friend Jimmy Swailes. A dark spot was merely an oil leak or a place where somebody broke a bottle of Pepsi. It's easier to forget a dark spot, and I desperately wanted to erase the memory of what had happened just hours before.

From their hiding-places in the weeds, katydids began singing their night songs. On this mournful occasion the high-pitched drone seemed to be whining, "Jim-my's dead, Jim-my's dead." I fought the urge to scream his name into the descending darkness; I wanted to call him back from wherever he had gone. Each time someone happened to pass by on the street, I imagined it was Jimmy coming back from the hospital morgue to tell me it had all been a terrible mistake. But the shadowy figures always walked by the house, disappearing into the twilight.

As the moon began to cast its feeble light, I went inside and climbed the stairs to a bedroom I shared with Fred. My brother was stretched crossways in the bed with one chubby leg hanging over the edge. I grabbed my pillow and the bedspread that had been kicked onto the floor. As a soft breeze rippled the tattered curtains, I made a comfortable nest in front of the window.

Merciful seeds of sleep germinated inside my consciousness almost immediately, intermingling with a fragmented swirl of the day's events. I kept seeing Jimmy's body, the Mexican's leering face, and the new basketball bouncing into the street. The images reappeared several times, until faces and figures began to blur and run together. Then, as oblivion began to cover me with its comfortable blanket, one last thought flickered. Jimmy had mentioned something about getting saved. Now, as before, I wondered what that meant. Saved? Saved from what? My final, fuzzy conclusion was that such a word had no meaning for Jimmy Swailes. He had not been saved at all. He had been killed!

IOWA

2

*T*wo days later I attended my first funeral. The afternoon was miserably hot. As Mom and I walked the five blocks to the funeral home, our clothes grew damp in all the usual places. Dad had declined to go, saying he wasn't much good at such affairs. Mom got mad and said he would have been plenty useful if the ceremony was a drunken wake for one of his tavern cronies. Had he been drinking, a fight would have followed; sober, he was no match for one of her rare displays of temper. He was content to stay clear of her until we left for the services.

It felt strange to be walking down the street beside my mother again. I hadn't done so in years. Yet, there was a comforting familiarity about the whole business. At thirteen, I was too old to hold her hand and too immature to take her arm. We simply walked, seldom speaking, her in a green dress that had been around a long time, and me in my good pants, white shirt, and Dad's wide brown tie that reached nearly to my waist.

Ziegenhorn's Funeral Parlor was a converted grocery store located directly across the street from Greenwood Cemetery. Old Man Ziegenhorn was one of McKinley's true characters, having married six times, with each spouse ending up in one of his discount plots. It was rumored he had recently purchased another section of ground to cover future marital plans. The only other mortuary in town was McGonigle—Craig, an establishment handling upper-class dead. Their ad in the Yellow Pages promised "Eternity with Elegance," while Ziegenhorn's merely mentioned having the cheapest rates in town. The McGonigle-Craig building resembled a castle; Ziegenhorn's place looked like a converted grocery store. McGonigle-Craig's setup had "class" written all over it. So did Ziegenhorn's, only it was preceded by the word "second."

There were always rumors floating around town concerning the strange little funeral director, and he didn't help matters any with his unusual behavior. A friend of Dad's used to dig graves for a living, and he claimed that Old Man Ziegenhorn always referred to dead people in unflattering terms such as "cold cuts," "canned goods," or "day-old bread." The gravedigger would be told by Ziegenhorn, "You'll have to work late tonight—I've got day-old bread to get into the ground before the weekend." When complaining about never getting any business from the affluent section of town, he would lament, "If I could just pick up a few of them expensive canned goods, I could retire in five years." To the public's face he called corpses the "deceased" or the "recently departed," but behind the scenes they were merely perishable items whose expiration date had come due.

Another strange habit he had was trying to convince the bereaved family not to bother using his hearse to transport the casket to the grave site. He insisted they could save money by having pallbearers carry the casket across Preemption Boulevard to its final resting-place. Skeptics maintained that he was less concerned with customer economics than his own convenience. Supposedly he also used the hearse to escort eligible ladies about town, and the back of the car was equipped to handle any opportunities which might present themselves during the course of a date. It was tiresome work to remove all his belongings every time some joker kicked the bucket just so a casket wouldn't have to be carried a block or so. Cold cuts should not take precedence over warm flesh!

Perhaps the most amazing rumor of the many that circulated around Old Man Ziegenhorn had him owning a chess set made from fingers and toes of past clientele. I wasn't sure I believed such a thing, but many people did. Mom knew a lady who talked to some guy who had an uncle claiming to have seen the gruesome figures one night while peeking through a window in one of the back rooms where Ziegenhorn lived. The man swore he had seen the amputated pawns and rooks, but it was hard to put too much faith in someone who made a habit of skulking around funeral parlors.

Our destination sat atop a high terrace, and the steps leading to it were intimidating. Whoever originally thought the location suitable for a grocery store deserved to go out of business. People were not anxious to carry their goods down those stairs, especially in Winter. Likewise, pallbearers couldn't be too happy at the prospect of transporting a heavy casket in such a manner, regardless of how it might benefit Ziegenhorn's nightlife!

Merely walking up the steps was no picnic either, as Mom and I soon discovered. The heat made it seem like an attempt to scale the Great Pyramid. We used the rickety handrailing, made from connecting sections of old waterpipe, to pull ourselves to the top. Halfway to to the summit I stomped a huge, brown beetle; it sounded like someone stepping on a potato chip. I felt no guilt over committing such a wanton act. If Jimmy had to be dead, why should a bug be allowed to live?

Shrubbery along the front of the building hung limply, as if in mourning. The air wasn't much cooler inside, but it was nice to be out of the sun's cruel glare. A ceiling fan turned slowly above our heads, and several flies were using it as a merry-go-round. Off to our right a door opened. A short, sweating usher asked us to please wait there while he carried a spray of flowers somewhere down the hall. Mom took hold of my shoulders, turning me toward her.

"Let me see if your hair is presentable."

Her breath was in my face. It smelled of cinnamon. I tried not to breathe at all because mine usually smelled like a sewer. With her fingers she pushed the most wayward strand of hair back upon my forehead, mentioning that I should have made a trip to the barbershop before attending this funeral. I was glad to have missed that opportunity; our barber had a way of making me look subhuman for nearly two weeks after each cutting. Besides, had I come to the funeral home freshly shorn, Old Man Ziegenhorn might have mistaken me for some of his day-old bread.

"This way, ma'am." The usher was back, wiping his neck with a handkerchief. He led us to a large, well-lighted room filled with metal folding chairs. A center aisle divided them. Clumps of widely-scattered humanity dotted both sections; there couldn't have been more than thirty people in the whole place. "Relatives or friends of the family?" asked the usher.

"Friends," said Mom.

"Very good. After you have viewed the casket, you may sit anywhere on the left."

Mom thanked him and bent over to sign the guest book. I took a quick look around. Nobody was familiar to me except Jimmy's mom and dad sitting in the first row to the right. Staring silently ahead, they appeared to be in shock. Their attention was focused upon a bronze casket sitting at the front of the room. At both ends of the casket, as well as behind it, were numerous rows of red and white floral tributes. The air was full of their fragrance and also the scratchy strains of "Beyond the Sunset" as somewhere out of sight a record machine played in a manner which went a long way toward explaining why Ziegenhorn's had the cheapest rates in town.

"Not too many people here," I said to Mom when she had finished writing.

"No, there aren't. But it's only quarter till . . . I'm sure there are more on the way."

We walked up the aisle toward the casket. I heard crying in the Relatives section, but didn't want to embarrass anyone by looking around. Mom's hand was on my shoulder, and I was glad to have it there because a sudden case of nerves possessed me. The thought of once again seeing Jimmy's dead body became more disturbing with each step. I remembered him in the street with a towel over his face. My stomach began to feel queasy. I walked with my head down, delaying eye contact as long as possible, but too soon we were at the casket. For a few more seconds I stared at the worn, red carpeting, then lifted my face to bid farewell to an old friend.

The walls of Jimmy's casket were lined with a satiny-looking material the color of doll flesh. A border of delicate tassels draped across each end. Gleaming brass handles hung on the outside, awaiting the sweaty palms of the men who would carry the casket to a prepared hole in the ground.

Mom touched a tissue to the corner of her eyes as I took the first hesitant look at the boy I used to know. I heard her sniffle, and

I had to concentrate hard on what was in front of me or else risk the shame of crying in public.

"He looks good, doesn't he," she said.

I nodded in agreement. But to be honest, he didn't look good at all. His skin appeared hard and cold, his hair looked too oily, and he seemed pitifully small for the blue suit he wore. Something else was wrong too, but for a while I couldn't pinpoint the problem. I thought about how Jimmy was supposed to look, going over him from top to bottom in my mind. It finally came to me: he wasn't wearing his glasses. Normally that would have been easily noticeable because the skin around his eyes was always pale compared to the rest of his face. But on a powdered, pallid corpse, there was no longer any difference in skin coloring. In life he was as blind as a mole without his glasses; now he was unaffected by their absence. I had to swallow hard several times.

Old Man Ziegenhorn positioned another spray of flowers just off to our left. "Terrible thing to happen to a young boy," he said to Mom.

"Yes, it is, Mr. Ziegenhorn."

The mousy little funeral director, whose normal expression reminded me of a man sniffing catfish bait, stuck his face close to mine. "We did a nice job on your friend, don't you think?"

"Nice job?"

"Oh my, yes! He was a sight when we first got him—so much damaged tissue and swelling, you understand. If I do say so myself, this is a masterful job of camouflaging the trouble spots. I wouldn't be surprised if McGonigle—Craig went with a closed-casket ceremony in a similar situation."

He was already moving away from us before the last few words were out of his mouth. Mom looked at me and rolled her eyes in amazement.

"That man is always advertising. Is it any wonder people talk about him the way they do?"

"Well, at least he didn't call Jimmy 'canned goods,'" I said.

No doubt Old Man Ziegenhorn was a fruitcake, but in his own special way he was also a comfort. His reputation and odd mannerisms were enough of a distraction to subtly divert some small portion of the grief and apprehension that were almost overwhelming at such times. Keeping an eye on him momentarily took away the pain of what lay in the bronze casket. The respite was brief, to be sure, but even the smallest drop of water is a comfort to those who thirst. Watching him strut down the aisle and disappear through a side door, I realized he was probably a decent guy and that all those rumors were just the products of overactive imaginations. Still, each time he came close to me, I instinctively put my hands in my pockets lest he get a good look at my thumbs.

After a final minute at the casket, Mom and I went over to Mr. and Mrs. Swailes to offer condolences. Jimmy's mother looked as if she hadn't eaten or slept since the accident. Her skin was sickly white except for dark areas around her eyes. The black dress she wore only made her coloring look worse—much like the underside of a frog. Jimmy's father sat expressionless, staring down at the floor. Mom squeezed Mrs. Swailes's arm.

"I'm so sorry this happened, Margaret. We all thought your Jimmy was such a fine boy. Is there anything we can do?"

The heartbroken woman shook her head as she valiantly fought to hold back the tears. Mom looked at me, as if it was my turn to speak. I wanted to say the right thing, but it was hard to know what was appropriate.

"Jimmy will always be my friend," I said. "I won't ever forget him."

For several seconds things were fine, but suddenly Mrs. Swailes broke down and began weeping. Mom leaned over, giving her a kiss on the cheek, then indicated to me with a movement of her head that we should leave. Mr. Swailes continued to stare at the floor.

We took seats halfway back on the left side. The room was filling up quickly now, as Mom had guessed it would.

"I didn't mean to make her cry," I said.

Mom gave me a one-armed hug. "It wasn't you. She's just full of pain, and it's liable to come out at any time. After this is all over, she will remember your words and cherish them." That made me feel better. Mom always knew how to get my chin off the ground when things weren't going right.

At five minutes past 2, the crackling record machine ceased its playing. A tall, bony-looking man dressed in black came striding up the center aisle. His face was grim, looking as if it had never experienced a smile. He had lost much of his hair, and the rest didn't appear worth keeping. Stepping behind a small wooden stand, which Old Man Ziegenhorn had placed in front of the casket, he pulled a black Bible from his coat pocket and motioned for everyone to rise.

"Bless this ceremony, Lord," he prayed, "in the name of the Father, the Son, and the Holy Ghost. Amen."

We sat down. The preacher wiped sweat from his forehead. The room felt like it was getting hotter by the minute.

"It is a sad thing indeed," he began, "when a young boy like this is taken from us. A boy who had his best years still ahead of him." Hearing those words, Mrs. Swailes lapsed into an hysterical outpouring of grief. A lady beside her whispered into her ear and patted her on the back. After a degree of control was restored, the preacher continued.

"Since Adam's fall it has been the plight of man to die. The Good Book says we were created from the dust of the earth, and a part of that same dust our bodies shall become after death. So it is with James Andrew Swailes."

I looked at Jimmy's dad. His cheeks were now wet.

"But this boy's spirit has gone from us now to a place where there are no more tears. He is in the presence of the Almighty God who has wrapped him in love like we could never do, no matter how hard we might try. He resides in those heavenly regions where all men long to be. So I say to you this day, weep not for James Swailes. It is a far better place he is in than he has ever been before."

The preacher continued the eulogy, but I heard no more. I was thinking of my pal Jimmy in Heaven with God. The man in black had made it all sound so good, so easy. I wanted it to be that way, for Jimmy's sake. But I kept remembering what Dad once said about Heaven being some myth that old people cling to when death is stepping on their heels. The preacher was certainly old, and it only made sense for him to speak of a Heaven for Jimmy if he expected to enter there himself sometime in the near future. But was there really a God at all? If so, why would He let Jimmy get killed in the first place? Going to a Heaven might be great for a dead person, but the family and friends left behind were invariably pulled through an emotional wringer. How were we supposed to know what was going on? Did Jimmy really make it or not? Why couldn't God just write a message in the sky saying everything was fine? The whole issue was very confusing, and the more I pondered, the less clear it all became.

"Let's go, Tommy," said Mom, urging me to stand and join the others as they moved toward the main exit. According to the clock on the wall, it was nearly 3. I felt as if I had been in a trance. Mom put a hand on my forehead. "Are you feeling alright?"

"I'm okay, but I was just wondering about something. Is there a God?"

The look she gave me was one of surprise and indecision. "I don't honestly know. I guess I've always hoped there was."

"Did He make Heaven?"

"If there is a Heaven, He made it."

"But you don't really know for sure if there is one or not?"

"How could anyone know for sure unless—oh, excuse us, sir!" Mom had accidentally bumped into an old man in a baggy brown suit. He gave us a cold scowl, then turned away. She blushed, and I silently vowed to give the guy an elbow if he crossed our path again.

We followed the crowd across Preemption Boulevard to the grave site for the burial ceremony. The sun was a probing yellow eye looking deep inside my baking brain as we walked among the headstones. I ran a finger over one gray granite marker and was surprised at its coolness. It was easy to imagine Jimmy resting in a dark, peaceful hole, covered by soft, green carpeting that kept out heat and noise and light. I almost envied his endless serenity.

Gentle hands removed the casket from the hearse. I was glad Jimmy's parents had decided to make use of the black 1956 Cadillac. It was only right. Jimmy deserved the best (although Ziegenhorn's best was oftentimes the worst).

As the six perspiring pallbearers positioned their load for its final descent, I saw several women crying, Mrs. Swailes included. Their sorrow filled the dead air with a heavy, penetrating gloom. The anguish of the moment plus the fierce heat combined to make every second of the service seem eternal. The preacher read from his Bible again, but I didn't listen. I had decided, during the brief walk from the funeral home, that the whole thing was ridiculous. There was no God and no Heaven. The preacher and all his words from the black book were nothing but smoke. It didn't make sense that a God would make people suffer the way we were suffering. He was either illusionary or idiotic; it didn't really matter which. I ejected Him from my mind like a spent shell casing from a rifle.

When the ordeal was finally over, Mom and I cut across the rear of the cemetery toward home. The grass was longer back there, and I walked slightly ahead of her to make certain no garter snakes lurked beneath the dandelions. Mom wasn't afraid of too many things, but the sight of a snake reduced her to a quivering mass. As we approached the small ravine that would connect us with Jackson Street, she was saying I never should have talked her into taking a shortcut. The ravine was probably crawling with snakes, she said. I was trying not to laugh, when a voice from behind us came wafting through the trees. We turned and saw someone coming our way, waving. It was Old Man Ziegenhorn.

"Hold up a minute," he called, "I got something for you."

A picture formed in my mind of him whipping out a sharp knife and removing our thumbs, right there on the outer fringes of Greenwood Cemetery. If Mom hadn't been with me, I might have panicked.

Ziegenhorn was panting like a pink-tongued dog by the time he reached us. He bent over, putting his hands on his knees.

"What is it, Mr. Ziegenhorn?" Mom asked, amused at his condition.

He held out his hand to me. "This belonged to young Swailes," he gasped. "His mother said it was very special to him and she wants the boy to have it."

From his small, moist palm I removed a silver ring. It was unfamiliar to me because I couldn't remember Jimmy ever wearing jewelry of any kind. There was an inscription inside. The words touched me in a manner which defied description and certainly explanation. They said, "I am the way, the truth, and the life."

• • • •

The next evening found me in the basement surrendering my army men to Fred. It hadn't been so long ago that I played with the green plastic figures for hours at a time. A vast wooden table with six legs thicker than my own was the battlefield on which I commanded my miniature military. Over the years I had conquered more enemies than Alexander, Napoleon, and Genghis Khan combined. It had all been great fun, but the green soldiers had now lost their appeal. Creating sound effects of ricocheting bullets, exploding bombs, or crashing planes no longer had much of a place in my life. Several months ago I had retired my regiments to a couple of boxes in the rear of a dingy closet; now I handed them over to a drooling Fred.

"I can't believe you're giving me all of this," he gushed as I issued him pile after pile of men and equipment.

"Just make sure you keep your mitts off my other stuff."

"Okay, Tommy."

I watched him position the soldiers in straight lines and speak military dialogue similar to what was heard each week on "Combat." He was such a dud, a thorn in the flesh I had carried for eight long years, spoiled like month-old milk and seeming to exist only to cause me aggravation and embarrassment. I couldn't go anywhere or do anything without him whining to be included. Mom always told me I should feel honored that he thought so much of my companionship. I didn't buy that idea. Does a dog feel honored because a tick latches onto him?

It didn't help that Fred was such a slob. He always had a snotty nose, junk between his teeth, or some kind of red, swollen bites with the tops scratched off. When I awoke each morning, the first sight to greet me was his fat face, both eyelashes decorated with yellow flakes and his chin coated with dried slobbers.

I didn't hate my brother, but I could have gotten along better as a single act. I needed him like Custer needed Little Bighorn. Such feelings forced me to avoid his company as much as possible, and that was one reason for giving him the soldiers. Normally I wouldn't give him anything other than a hard time, but this evening there was important business to take care of, and I didn't want him tagging along. The new playthings would occupy his dull mind long enough for me to sneak away.

There was another reason for surrendering the soldiers. I had recently become aware of a strange emptiness growing inside me.

At times it was just an annoying twinge, but at its worst the thing gnawed away like a starving rat. I sensed a gaping black hole that could never be filled.

I considered going to my parents about the problem, but how could they be expected to explain something I couldn't even describe? Had I mentioned the void eating at my gut, Mom would likely have prescribed a generous dose of cod-liver oil, and Dad would have told me that the empty spot in my head must have dropped a couple feet. Better to keep things to myself than have ridicule added to my other burdens.

But at night, in the darkness of our room, a feeling of despair invaded my soul, and not one thing in the world seemed worthwhile. The side of my bed became the edge of an abyss. In moments of desperation I threw in my hopes, beliefs, and all the things dearest to me, but I never heard them hit bottom. I cried a lake of blanket-smothered tears. Nothing satisfied the monster.

Now, by giving up a childhood treasure, I had conceded youth as well. My hope was that maybe this wretched condition was merely a temporary aberration of pubescence which the onset of manhood would vanquish forever. The quicker I grew up, the quicker I might become free.

Dad yelled for me to come upstairs. He was sitting at the kitchen table behind an ashtray full of cigarette butts and a can of Schlitz beer. The room smelled like a tavern.

"Where you been?" he asked, as if I had been gone a year.

"Basement."

His brown hair was pointing in all directions, like some greasy weathervane. The clothes he wore appeared never to have felt the touch of an iron. His red-rimmed eyes wandered up and down my frame, finally focusing upon my right hand.

"What's that ring?"

"It was Jimmy's. His parents wanted me to have it."

"Lets see."

Reluctantly I slipped the ring off and put it in his unsteady hand. He examined it and tried to read the inscription. Alcohol did not have a positive effect upon his vision.

"What's it say?" he finally demanded.

"I am the way, the truth, and the life."

He looked at me as if I had uttered Mandarin Chinese.

"Huh?"

I repeated the words.

This time he laughed. "What a stupid thing to have on a ring. Where'd he get it, out of a gumball machine?"

"I doubt it."

"Well, what's it supposed to mean?"

"Something religious, I think . . . I'm not sure."

He tossed the ring onto the table, lifted his can of beer, and sucked it dry. His Adam's apple bounced like a bobber in choppy water. I put the ring back on my finger and moved toward the back door.

"You ain't going anywhere," he said grabbing my arm.

"I'm supposed to meet Hippo Reeves in five minutes."

"You don't do nothing unless I say so." He squeezed my arm until it hurt, but I stared at him like I didn't know he was touching me.

Water was forming in the corners of my eyes when he finally released his grip. He told me to get him another beer from the refrigerator. I did so, tossing it at him in the same careless manner that he had thrown Jimmy's ring. He made an awkward catch and then used the pointed end of a bottle opener to make two triangular holes in the can. All else was momentarily forgotten as he gulped down his beloved brew. I looked at him sitting there in such a sorry state and wondered how he came to be this way. Pictures of my dad in his younger days held the image of a handsome man. There had been a sparkle in his eyes accompanied by a confident smile. Both had long since vanished.

"You go see Hippo for a while," he finally mumbled, "but stay close. This might be a bad night to be out and about."

"Why's that?"

"I heard there's a lot of bad blood about that Mexican running down a white kid. Some guys I know say that a few beaners might get their heads broke before this is all through. Anything could happen."

Dad always called Mexicans "beaners," or some other derogatory name. Jews were "kikes," Italians were "wops," and everyone was something—except the Kanes. I had never heard it called racial prejudice, but even then I knew it was wrong, though I was too chicken—and too upset over Jimmy—to do anything about it.

"You gonna help?" I asked him.

He gave a bleary-eyed shake of the head. "They don't need me just to crack a few skulls. I'm too old for that stuff anymore."

I was disappointed although not surprised at his lack of interest in gaining a measure of revenge for what had been done to Jimmy. To him the incident had merely been "a bad deal for the Swailes kid." To me it had been a heinous act for which no punishment could be too severe. Dad could stay home and drink away any feelings of obligation that pricked his conscience, but not me. Tom Kane had a plan for retribution.

• • • •

Hippo Reeves was finishing off a huge sack of potato chips when I met him at the Dillon Street railroad crossing. He wore a green sleeveless shirt and faded blue jeans, which seemed to be the only things I had seen him wear since he moved to our neighborhood four years ago. My second-best friend was a large, round guy with numerous folds of skin to accommodate future growth. He had a fat face and an upturned nose featuring nostrils big enough to insert dimes. I knew this to be true because I had seen him do it during recess when we were in grade school. After that I was reluctant to accept small coins from him for fear they had been somewhere other than his pocket.

"Did you bring the stuff?" I asked him.

He pointed to a can of paint and two ragged brushes stacked next to a tree stump. "You gonna tell me what it's all about, or is it a military secret?"

"Payback for what happened to Jimmy," I said.

He wadded up the empty chip bag and flipped it over his shoulder. "I don't get the connection."

"Look, Hippo, the name of the bum who killed Jimmy is Carlos Montez. The newspaper gave his address, and we're personally going to deliver a written message to his home . . . with brushes and paint so everyone can see it."

"I don't see what good that will do," Hippo said. "This Montez is in jail, and he probably don't own the place anyway, so what does he care?"

I picked up the can of paint, leaving the brushes for him. "I don't know what good it will do. Maybe it's totally stupid, but I have to try something or I'll go nuts. Every time I think about that Mexican laughing at what he did to Jimmy, I want to scream. This paint job won't help Jimmy, but it might do me some good. So let's go."

We slid down the pile of crushed rock that formed the base of the track bed. This particular set of tracks, built unusually high because of annual seepage from the nearby Mississippi, skirted the eastern edge of McKinley and effectively shielded us from being seen by anyone on the town side. We moved swiftly for about six blocks until the tracks and a paralleling road diverged around a broad expanse of rough grassland. Several hundred yards beyond, on the backside of the clearing, were three short, dead-end streets. The one in the middle, named after James Madison, was our destination.

Hippo and I moved closer. The red-orange sun appeared larger than normal as it dipped beneath the top branches of distant trees. We ran bent-over, like guys with bellyaches, between various pieces of junk scattered behind the last house on Madison Street. There was a tilted, rusting stove with a bird's nest hanging from one burner. From there we moved to a pile of tires and then onward to an overturned wooden cart. The house was now very close.

"You sure that's the Mexican's place?" asked Hippo.

"Don't worry about it. Give me your knife."

Hippo tried jamming a thick hand into the back pocket of his faded jeans, but it became stuck. Like a dog chasing its tail, he kept turning in circles, looking over his shoulder at the problem area. "I'm caught," he yelled.

I put my hand over his mouth, barely spanning the gap. "Hold it down, man. Let's don't blow this before we even start."

He relaxed enough for me to remove his hand from the pocket and insert my own. After a brief struggle I extricated the knife and then used the blade to pry off the paint can lid. The color inside was red. Blood-red.

"What are we supposed to write?" Hippo asked when I handed him one of the brushes.

"Anything, as long as it embarrasses the tamale family."

We were dripping sweat, and my heart was suddenly trying to push its way through my rib cage. It would have been smart to rest a while, but darkness was fast approaching. On hands and knees we crossed the short space from the overturned cart to the back of the house. I didn't need the full light of day to see that the place was a dump. The backdoor screen hung in tatters, and the step leading to it was nothing but a broken cement block. Two overflowing garbage cans, minus lids, served as a restaurant for several hundred flies. They buzzed and darted angrily as we crawled by. A television blared inside. A baby was crying.

"Start paintin' right here," I whispered, pointing to the wall space between a window and the corner of the house. I dipped my brush into the can and began printing a large M.

"What's that gonna be?" asked Hippo.

"Murderer."

"Oh."

He was on all fours, staring straight ahead, trying to think of something to write on the house. His blank facial expression reminded me of a cow in a field. For a few minutes he watched me work, offering an occasional criticism.

"Better make that D bigger, else it won't fit too good with them other letters."

"You dumb jerk," I hissed in his face, "this isn't a penmanship class. Just get busy . . . And keep a lookout in case anybody shows up."

"Gotcha."

After finishing several suitable words, I checked on Hippo's progress.

"How's that?" he grinned, pointing proudly at his work. It read: "I killed Jimmy Swailes."

"Fantastic," I said.

There was only one tiny window on that side of the house, so we had plenty of room to continue our literary endeavor. I wrote, "Mexicans are greasy," and Hippo painted, "Tacos go home," but he spelled tacos with a k. We added a few obscenities for emphasis, then Hippo drew a swastika for reasons known only to his warped mind. The paint was almost gone, so we decided to save whatever remained for the front of the house. It was getting hard to see.

I had just made my first stroke beside the front window when a fat Mexican woman and a young boy came screaming at us, brandishing brooms. The woman wore an orange dress big enough to cover a Cub Scout troop. Yelling words I couldn't understand, she went after Hippo, who was closest to her. Just as he started to run, her broom whacked across his shoulders, sending him somersaulting to the lawn. The boy, who looked to be ten or eleven, wore cut-off jeans and an unbuttoned white shirt that trailed behind him as he ran toward me. Without thinking, I stood my ground and swung the can of paint like a battle-ax. The kid dropped to the ground, the loose shirttail partially covering his face.

"Let's beat it," I yelled, turning in the direction of the tracks.

Hippo tried to obey, but each time he started to get up, the woman clubbed him and put him back on his belly. I wanted to run, but something about the Mexican boy drew me toward him. Ignoring the chaos around me, I bent over to take a closer look in the faint light. Hair on the back of my neck snapped to attention when I saw he had blood all over his chest and head. It was beginning to soak through the portion of shirt draped over his face. I screamed like the heroine in a cheap horror movie as the body momentarily became that of Jimmy Swailes lying in a hot street under a bloody towel. Now, as before, I was unable to move.

"Roberto," cried the woman when she saw her boy was down. The broom fell from her hand as she left Hippo to go to her son. My buddy took advantage of her absence to finally regain an upright position and begin a full retreat. Both he and the woman were running in the same direction. It was a dead heat until she pulled up beside the boy. Hippo rumbled past without even noticing me. After a few more strides the darkness absorbed him.

In the worst way I wanted to be leaving with him, but he would have had to carry me on his back for that to be possible. With my nonfunctioning body, all I could do was watch as the woman lifted her son's bloody head to her lap. He looked dead. I could almost feel cuffs clamping onto my wrists as the police hauled us up on a murder charge. The woman massaged the boy's forehead, gently tapping his cheek with her hand. She wept. Then, to our great surprise and utter joy, he suddenly sat up and rubbed the side of his head. The woman said something to him in short, sharp syllables, and he answered in the same manner. She ran a finger through the blood on his face, smelling it. Looking around, she picked up a wet brush and began to giggle. The kid laughed too. I laughed loudest of all as sweet truth forced its way into my confused brain. The kid wasn't really bleeding; like the house, he had only been painted. No prison term for Tom Kane after all.

My legs were now operational, and I took off after Hippo at half-speed. Visibility was so poor that anything faster would have constituted suicide. My partner in crime was waiting by the pile of tires. "I thought you got caught," he said, breathing heavily.

Before I could answer, the sound of a siren came to us from not too far away. Immediately we charged the tracks. Hippo led the way with me on his heels wanting to pass, but afraid of what might be waiting in the shadows. I was blind except for barely being able to distinguish his silhouette against the faintest possible glimmer along the horizon. I might as well have shut my eyes and followed the sound of him sucking air.

The siren got louder. I sensed the tracks were close by and eased up to avoid making footprints on Hippo's back. Then, for no apparent reason, the silhouette rose a couple of feet into the air and dropped down again. I had about half a second to consider the cause for such a movement before my legs were cut from under me by a tree stump. That unexpected obstacle made it possible for me to execute a full flip with a partial twist. I landed on my side, mowing grass for several feet. There was instant pain in my shins and left shoulder, but I had no time to fret over minor injuries. Spitting grass, I was right back on my feet. In another few seconds we scrambled over the tracks and down the backside to safety. The danger of being discovered was over now, but we kept moving at a good clip just the same.

Fifteen minutes later we were inside my garage, feeling rather smug. Sitting on overturned tomato hampers, beneath a bare bulb, we listened for approaching sirens. The atmosphere around us was like that of a dungeon. The cracked cement floor, always damp, was covered with an assortment of slimy creatures appreciating a moist environment. The air smelled like a wet catcher's mitt. Moths crawled outside the window, pressing against the glass, eager to join those fortunate few inside who were circling the dim light. Cobwebs connected the corners of the garage and laced its upper regions; their sticky gray filaments were speckled with carcasses of careless insects. Such morbid surroundings were hardly conducive to happiness, but with each passing minute our spirits soared ever higher. We had pulled it off!

Hippo rubbed his sides and back. "Man, I am one sore sucker. I think that big mama was tryin' to make a pie outta me with that broom."

"I bet my legs feel just as bad," I said.

"What happened to you?"

"I didn't see that stump you jumped over . . . Almost broke me in half."

Hippo laughed as we compared bruises and abrasions. But then he plopped back down on his hamper, a look of wide-eyed shock spreading across his face.

"We forgot the brushes," he mumbled. "They got our prints all over 'em. We're dead!"

"You're right," I said, kicking the wall in disgust. "The last time I saw your brush, that woman was holding it."

"Then we gotta go back," Hippo said.

I knew that was a rotten idea. "No way! We don't dare go back to the scene. All we can do is wait, keep our mouths shut, and hope our prints got smeared. Anyway, how do we even know the cops in this town can lift a fingerprint? Half of them have trouble directing traffic on a one-way street. I say all we have to do is wait and act like nothing happened."

Hippo thought for a moment and saw the sense of my suggestion. We mumbled a promise to keep quiet, then separated to our homes for the night. As he left the garage, I had a feeling that Hippo's concern about being discovered by a police investigation would be short-lived. He would sleep the sleep of one who seldom worries. I knew I, however, would probably stew until the pink of dawn.

I don't know what time I finally got to sleep, but it seemed only thirty seconds later that Mom shook me and said I must come downstairs to eat breakfast with the family. When I complained of being too tired, she let the ragged window shade snap upward around the roller. Painful sunlight flooded the room. My shoulder throbbed from last night's tumble, and my mouth tasted like Fred had used it to store his dirty socks.

"Five minutes, Tommy, or I'll start scratching."

When it came to making sure sleepy family members climbed out of bed on time, Mom had the perfect method: she would scratch her fingernails across the door. Foggy-brained offenders always had both feet on the floor before those agonizing nails could begin their second run. I was tired, but not enough to risk hearing that horrible sound.

I staggered to the dresser and pulled out a clean pair of jeans. Dancing along the floor and trying to shove a foot through the proper opening absorbed most of my available mental powers, but a thought was born amid the chaos. Eat breakfast with the family? Was that what Mom had said? Such a phrase implied that Dad would be joining us. For many reasons, including working a rotating shift, he was very seldom around during the morning meal. I had no idea why he was gracing us with his presence on this particular day; I only wished he had been working so I could have stayed in bed.

"Well hello, sunshine," Dad said when I entered the kitchen.

Only an alcohol-induced euphoria or unexpected good fortune could have caused him to greet me in such a manner, and taverns weren't open at this early hour. He was clean-shaven and wearing a freshly-ironed shirt. I wished my own appearance had been a little more presentable. There was a distinct possibility I resembled yesterday's scrambled eggs.

"How many pancakes can you eat, Tommy?" Mom asked while pouring batter into a black skillet.

It was hard not to laugh when she asked that question. Mom was a fine cook, but she had a problem with pancakes. She made them so big and thick, they resembled cushions. When she laid one on a plate, the plate disappeared. I could pour half a bottle of syrup over one of those monsters and it would be absorbed in a matter of seconds. Fred or I could battle a single pancake for most of an hour, feel completely bloated, and still be only halfway finished. When my friends talked about eating half a dozen pancakes for breakfast, I thought them to be liars. I was twelve befoɪe ever finding out that not all pancakes were the size of garbage can lids.

"Uh, just one please," I told her.

"I've got plenty of batter if you want more."

"Give the poor kid a break, Louise," Dad said. "If he ate two of those things, his legs would start to bow."

I laughed out loud, and Mom even chuckled a little as she slapped one of her creations onto my plate. Fred still had a lot of pancake left in front of him. The defeated look on his face told me he was one or two bites from the end of the line.

"Guess they really had a wild time last night in Little Mexico," Dad said, buttering a piece of toast.

"What happened?" Mom asked.

"Somebody painted up Carlos Montez's place and beat up one of his kids."

My throat closed tightly around my first bite of breakfast, and I choked. Mom thumped me on the back. "Good heavens, Thomas Kane, when will you learn not to gulp your food?"

Dad gave me a curious look, then continued his story.

"I was talking to Andy Sloan about it, and he says Montez's wife told the cops it was a whole gang that did it. They wrote all over the house, and then when the woman and kid came out to stop them, the kid got crunched over the head with a pipe or something. I'd say it took some kind of nerve to pull that off right down there in pickle-picker territory."

I dropped my eyes to the load on my plate, shoving enough food into my mouth to cover any trace of a smile that might have been forming. It was fun to hear Dad talk about our adventure as if it had been some great deed. The urge to reveal my participation in the glorious event was overwhelming, but I just kept cramming my face full of pancake. I understood now how hard it must have been for Zorro and Superman to keep their true identity a secret.

"I think the whole business is just shameful," Mom said. "Those people have enough on their minds without trouble like that."

Dad didn't agree. "Don't go feeling sorry for 'em . . . They're only Mexicans."

"They are human beings!"

"That's never been proved," he said, grinning at his own joke.

Nobody spoke for a while, but Mom rattled dishes and slammed cupboard doors. Whenever she was too upset to talk, the most noticeable symptom of her anger was much banging and crashing in the kitchen. Nothing cured her condition except the passage of time, so Dad read the paper and Fred stared at the wall. I hacked away at the pancake and tried, with reasonable subtlety, to return the flow of conversation to last night's incident.

"Did they ever figure out who did the painting?"

"Not that I heard," Dad said, "but they found some brushes that were left behind. I figure maybe a fingerprint will be taken up if they get lucky."

My heartbeat went to triple digits, and sweat droplets trickled between my protruding shoulder blades. What would Mom think if she found out her son had taken part in something she obviously found revolting? The pancake refried itself inside my stomach as I waited for more bad news, but Dad changed the subject.

"Well, it's time to talk about more pleasant things. How about taking a trip to Missouri?"

Fred stuck his head out of a fog. "Missouri! Oh boy! We can go see Huckleberry Hound. My teacher says he lives there."

"I think you mean Huckleberry Finn, dear," Mom said.

"Does he got a raft?"

"I believe so."

"Then that's him." My brother looked as if his brain had been removed and put inside a fruit jar for safekeeping.

"Why are we going to Missouri?" I asked.

Mom scraped the remainder of Fred's pancake into an empty milk carton. "Your father's relatives are from Missouri," she explained. "They haven't seen you since you were a baby, and they've never seen Freddy. We got a letter last week inviting us to come visit them. Your father tried to get time off, but his boss said things were too busy for anyone to leave. But now, with the trouble last night, he'll be able to go after all."

"What does last night have to do with what goes on at Dad's work?"

"Let's just say it caused a spark that lit a fire," Dad said. "After that gang did its business at Little Mexico, the word got back to some of the greasers down at the plant. Next thing we know, the generator room is burning like crazy, and before the firemen can get it out, most of the main wiring is ruined. I don't know what those Mexican bums had in mind, but all they did was slit their own throats. We'll be shut down at least two weeks, maybe more. I can use my vacation time and it won't cost me anything, but they're out of luck. Serves 'em right."

"Where's Missouri at?" interrupted Fred.

"It's right below Iowa," Dad said.

"Are we sitting on it?"

"No. I meant right below us on a map. After we get past Iowa, then we come to Missouri, just like after our house we get to Old Man Carver's place. See what I mean?"

Fred gave a vague nod, and Dad laughed. That was unusual because silly questions or improper reactions to his answers were often rewarded with a smack on the head or an invitation to leave the room. I found his jovial disposition rather unsettling.

"I want you to stay close to home today, Tommy," Mom said. "There's plenty of packing to get done before tomorrow morning."

"Tomorrow morning!"

"Yes, and I'll never make it if I don't start right now. Freddy, you come upstairs and we'll get your clothes sorted out."

Soon Dad and I had the room to ourselves. I stabbed at the "pillow" in front of me. He sipped his coffee, staring thoughtfully in my direction.

"You look a little ragged this morning, son," he said.

"Tired, I guess."

"Been getting enough sleep?"

"Oh, yeah . . . I think it's just the hot weather."

He pointed a finger. "That must be what caused the red stuff on your neck . . . The heat I mean. It looks like some sort of rash."

Without thinking, I ran my hand along the side of my neck. "I don't feel anything."

"Don't it itch?"

"Uh uh."

"Well, take a look in the mirror and see what you think it is."

I pushed away from the table and went to a mirror on the back of a closet door in the next room. One glance told me that disaster might be just ahead: the right side of my neck was smudged with red paint.

"I don't think it's a rash," I called out to Dad.

"What about measles?"

"Already had two kinds of measles."

"Well, keep an eye on it in case it gets any worse. We don't want to export any diseases to Missouri."

"Okay." I couldn't believe he wasn't going to push the issue any farther than that. All I needed to do was get past him to the bathroom and wash off the evidence before anyone got too good a look.

"What about your breakfast?" Dad asked as my foot hit the first step.

"I'm not really too hungry."

"Then scrape your plate and put things away, so your mother won't have to do it later."

Without appearing to hurry, I cleared my place at the table, keeping my right side turned away from him. When everything had been taken care of, I again headed toward the stairs.

"Was it you or Hippo that hit the Mexican kid?" Dad asked.

"It was m—" I stood there with my mouth hanging open, like the fool that I was.

"Sit down," he ordered. I obeyed. "You guys took a big chance last night."

"We just wanted to do something for Jimmy."

"Yes, but what if you'd got picked up by the law? Your mother would have went to an early grave."

"We didn't think about getting caught, I guess."

He rubbed his chin and leaned back on the chair, staring at the ceiling as if it was a giant cue card containing his next line. "I suppose what happened last night is water under the bridge, so we'll forget about it. As far as them Mexicans go, I wouldn't care if they all got conked in the head, just as long as you didn't get in trouble and cause your mother any pain. But I don't want you getting in any deeper than you already are. Let the ones who were hurt by Montez be responsible for their own payback from here on. Clear?"

"All right . . . but there's still a problem."

"What?"

"The brushes. If they do get our prints, what then?"

Dad laughed from deep inside his chest, shaking his head. "First of all, the cops in McKinley probably couldn't get prints off a finger, let alone a slimy brush. Second, you've never had your prints recorded, so how would anyone know if they belonged to you or a million other guys?"

I hadn't thought of that. They couldn't match our prints because there was nothing to compare them with. I was so happy I could almost have given Dad a hug, but sanity returned before I did anything too stupid. I was anxious to call Hippo and pass on the good news.

"I'm going to be on the phone a while," I said.

"You're going to be cleaning out the car," he corrected me. "All the stuff you need is already on the back porch." He watched me to see if there was going to be a protest, but I wasn't about to blow everything by complaining.

"Okay, just let me get on some shoes." I sat down and loosened the dirty strings of my tennis shoes while he lit a cigarette and blew a smoke ring.

"Actually, I'm kinda proud of what you did last night," he said.

"Really?"

"Yep. It took guts, and I know it was done for a friend."

"I figured you'd be mad."

"Long as you didn't get caught, that's all I care about. Mexicans in this town need to be taught not to mess with whites. We got plenty of them down at the plant that need to be showed the big picture. Your paint job might get it done. In a couple days there could be a war going on in this town, and we'll be far enough away not to have to worry. But like I said before, you're finished with it. You've done your part."

As he walked past me, heading upstairs, he playfully pulled the lobe of my ear. He hadn't done that in years. It made me feel strange.

I spent the rest of the morning working on the car and congratulating myself for the fine work done at the Battle of Little Mexico. The stiffness in my shoulder and the discoloration on my shins were proud reminders that I had answered the call to service. A fallen comrade's memory had been honored; one small measure of revenge had been gained. There would be more, regardless of promises mumbled to my dad.

The sun moved higher in the sky, warming the air and causing

my ego to expand. I felt heroic. I daydreamed about standing at the
Alamo, alongside Davy Crockett, fighting legions of Joses and
Chicos until death took me. Davy would fire "Old Betsy," and I
would swing a paint can as the piles of mustachioed bodies formed
around us. I was Terrible Tom Kane, the scourge of Mexicans everywhere, a fighting machine, a shaft of cold steel who left victims
bloodied and fearful!

Such wild thoughts as those were cultivated and fertilized in
my mind the rest of that day and late into the night. But with each
passing hour the satisfaction they provided grew smaller. The
seeds of revenge had indeed borne first fruit, and the harvest was
bountiful. However, in the middle of such abundance the empty
place inside me was unappeased, and the hole grew larger. Staring
at the stars from my bedroom window, I wondered where it was
all going to end. Could nothing in the world fill that gap? Was
there any light in the universe powerful enough to illuminate the
expanding darkness in my soul? Despite my shame at being so
weak, I moved closer to Fred and slept with one arm draped
across his bare chest.

• • • •

The eastern sky was just beginning to flaunt its orange and
pink splendor when Mom rousted Fred and me from our entangle-
ments among the damp sheets. Fred's legs weren't functioning too
well, so she walked him around the room a couple of times to has-
ten the awakening process. We had taken showers the night before,
and the clothes we were to wear hung from hooks on the closet
door. The shirt I put on stuck to my skin immediately. Sliding into
my socks required Houdini-like contortions.

Downstairs I found Dad pacing the kitchen floor, smoking one
cigarette after another. He yelled at me to quit standing around
looking stupid, quit watching him, get busy and eat, and whatever
else came to mind. The cigarette in his face bobbed with every syl-
lable. Smoke curling from the corners of his mouth was sucked
back into his nostrils with each inhalation. He reminded me of
Fred's old wind-up rabbit when its mainspring had been twisted
too tightly. Instead of completing its customary hop across the

floor, the toy simply flipped into the air and landed on its side—a pitiful display of too much inner tension.

Dad wasn't much of a traveler. His idea of a big trip was going to a bar across town instead of one down the street. I knew from past experience that the journey ahead would be miserable if he didn't get calmed down before we left. When his back was turned, I poured the contents of a cereal bowl into my mouth and went to help Mom load the car. She was in the front room checking her list against a pile of unmatched suitcases and frayed clothes bags.

"Where's your father?" she asked.

"He's in the—"

Just then Dad came out of the kitchen like a bull out of a chute. "We're taking too much junk," he complained after surveying the luggage pile. "When I was in the army, we took care of a whole company with less stuff than this."

As was generally her way, Mom ignored him and continued her business. She often took verbal abuse from Dad far beyond the limits most people would endure, seldom complaining. (Occasionally he touched a spot of vulnerability. Then Mom would cut him down. She didn't scream or get hysterical, like other women I had seen; her eyes would narrow to slits, and she would speak through bared teeth. At that point Dad usually backed off, letting things cool a bit.) Now, as we began loading the trunk, he continued yelling about the quantity of items going to Missouri. I had a feeling Mom was approaching the breaking-point.

When the last bag had been jammed into half the necessary space, she tried several times to close the trunk lid. It kept popping open.

"Figures," sneered Dad. "You got everything in there but the furnace. We might as well rent a truck."

"See if you can close it, please," Mom said.

"Well, I ain't Superman. Nobody but him is going to get the lid down on all this junk. I don't know what you want from me, woman."

Mom turned to him, her eyes like the edges of quarters.

"Nobody knows better than me that you're not Superman. I could be blind, deaf, and dumb, but I'd still know you're not Superman. What I want you to be is a regular man and carry your share of the load. Just once!"

She slammed the trunk viciously. It remained shut. Dad's mouth fell open like an oven door. His complexion assumed the appearance of one who had spent a week wandering the Sahara. He muttered something about double-checking the house, then hurried from Mom's presence. I felt like either laughing or cheering, but her eyes were still too narrow to risk being the recipient of any leftover hostility.

Things slowed down for a while after that. Mom went back inside, and Fred slumped in the porch swing like a pile of wet laundry. I decided to cut through a neighbor's yard to say good-bye to Hippo. Except for a short phone call, I hadn't talked with him since the Battle of Little Mexico. He didn't even know I was leaving town.

When I peeked into his window, I saw him sprawled across the bed.

"Hippo!" He was snoring. I scratched the screen with my fingernails. A small vapor of rust dust floated lazily through the wire barrier into the room. "Hey, Hippo. Wake up, you lazy bum."

"Go 'way," he said hoarsely.

"We need you for the game," I said.

"Game?" In seconds he was out of bed, pulling on a rumpled pair of jeans with holes in both knees. "I musta overslept. Stupid clock says it's only ten after 6."

"The clock's right."

"Sure it is."

"There's no game, Hippo. It's early morning. I just wanted you to wake up so I could say good-bye."

"No game? Good-bye?" He quit moving, and as soon as he did, sleep began recapturing his brain.

"I'm going to Missouri for a couple weeks."

"No lie? Your old man finally kicked you out, huh?"

"Actually we're going to visit some of my dad's relatives down there. And I could use the dollar you borrowed off me for swimming that time."

"Oh yeah, I almost forgot about that," he said, kicking the jeans into a corner. "Tell ya what, I'll pay it back tomorrow."

"I won't be here tomorrow, lunkhead. We're leaving right now."

Hippo hit the bed like a falling tree. "Then I'll settle up when ya get back."

"C'mon! I might need that money while I'm on the road."

"Good night," he said, rolling over and revealing sunburned shoulders.

The car horn was honking.

"I'll take care of you in two weeks," I yelled. He only giggled. Or perhaps he was snoring again.

I only took thirty seconds to get home, but Dad spent the next ten minutes chewing me out for leaving my post. While he ranted, Mom studied a roadmap and Fred grinned at me from across the backseat. My brother enjoyed seeing me squirm.

When the lecture was finally over, Dad backed the car across the front lawn, down over the curb, and into the street. Mom said we were ruining the grass. Dad said we would have ruined our backs if he hadn't pulled up close to the house to load all that luggage. While they argued the point, I looked out the side window at the faded stain on the pavement where Jimmy had died. By the time we returned, the spot would likely be gone. I looked at our shabby house and then at the one next door where Old Man Carver sat on his porch in a dirty shirt spitting into a coffee can. A dog barked close by, and a man's voice hollered for it to shut up. I thought of Hippo lying in his bed, and of the fresh mound of dirt at Greenwood Cemetery. I realized that I was very anxious to leave it all behind.

MISSOURI

Our car was a big, black Buick Roadmaster. It was an eleven-year-old monstrosity whose color, shape, and huge chrome grill put me in mind of a misshapen rubber boot with a single, oversized silver buckle on the toe. The car ran reasonably well during warm weather, but with the first severe drop in temperature all systems went into hibernation and it remained in the garage until Spring.

I didn't know exactly how we came to own such a machine. Dad simply disappeared for a few days and then came back driving a car that looked like it was destined for a demolition derby. When I asked him where he got it, he would only say it wasn't stolen if that's what I meant. I told him that wasn't what I meant at all, but he volunteered no further information. My father could be vague when it suited him.

Two hours south of McKinley, the car's black exterior was absorbing the sun's rays and transferring their warmth to the passengers. Scorching heat from the motor radiated through the fire wall as well, slowly dry-cooking us. We had all the windows down, but a 95-degree breeze does little to revive a wilted spirit. Dad's shirt was already soaked. Worse, his mood was explosive; the smallest thing might set him off. Like I said, he wasn't much of a traveler under the best of conditions, and after sweating for over a hundred miles he had the disposition of a Tyrannosaurus Rex.

"I can't believe you're thirty-four years old and don't drive a car," he said to Mom as if he had just then discovered she couldn't operate a motor vehicle. "A man drives halfway across the state and can't even take a break because his wife don't drive. Why am I so lucky?"

Mom ignored him and continued reading a confessions magazine. The caption above her story said something about "backseat bingo." A year earlier I might have wondered how players were able to keep their chips from sliding off the cards while riding in the backseat of a car.

Seeing he was wasting his breath on my mother, Dad looked in the rearview mirror for easier prey. I happened to glance his direction and quickly turned away, but we had been eyeball to eyeball for a fraction of a second. That was all he needed.

"What's your trouble, hotshot?"

When selected to serve as scapegoat, I was usually referred to as "hotshot" or "bigshot." Those names irritated me, often tempting disrespectful answers to escape from my mouth. One formed on my lips at that very moment and would certainly have been spoken had Fred not announced he was in urgent need of a bathroom. Dad's neck turned a deeper shade of red.

"You were supposed to take care of that before we left home!"

"I did," Fred whimpered, "but that was a long time ago."

"Lousy brat."

Fred sniffled, and I tried comforting him by making a pouting face and pointing a derisive finger. This prompted him to begin full-scale crying operations. Dad strangled the steering wheel. Mom closed her magazine and turned around in the seat.

"Let's be a big boy, Freddy."

"Nobody likes me."

"Of course they do. It's just that we're all hot and tired. July is not the best time to be heading south."

Dad gave her a blank stare. A cigarette hung from his mouth, and his expression reminded me of Humphrey Bogart.

"Look, woman, I didn't pick when we were supposed to come down here."

"I know that, dear. I just said it was a poor time to be heading south. I didn't mean it was your fault."

The relentless heat melted any further attempts at conversation, although Fred occasionally sighed to remind us he was in considerable pain. The narrow blacktop highway twisted through an endless green sea of corn and soybean fields. For the first few miles Mom had pointed out to Fred the "horsies," the "cute little piggies," and each "pretty red barn." Now we passed them in silence. It might have just been the hot weather, or perhaps Mom had finally realized what I knew all along: that each place was just another stupid farm and there was nothing at all special about the horses, pigs, or red barns. None of them mattered. The only things of consequence were the advancing of the odometer and escaping the unmerciful heat.

The farmland finally gave way to a town called Bloomington. It was smaller than McKinley, consisting mainly of a square built around a courthouse. As the Buick slowed down and eased into a gravel driveway to our left, I saw a neat-looking brick building with three oval windows in front. The name PALACE was above the knotty pine door.

"I need a beer," Dad said, "so we might as well grab a sandwich and use the toilets."

Fred was out the door like Man O' War out of the starting gate, but he had forgotten his shoes. The pain of gravel gouging his soft feet made him forget his other problem. While he limped back to the car, the rest of us got out and stretched cramped muscles. Mom stared down at her brown slacks.

"This place looks a little ritzy. I wish I had worn a dress."

"You women really kill me," Dad said, "always worrying about what to wear. Forget what people might think—just walk in the joint and feel good about it."

"Well, maybe you're right."

Anticipating an air-conditioned haven, we hurried toward the front door. Three of us walked in the normal manner; one hopped and stumbled, trying to jam shoes onto his feet without untying the strings.

"If there's only one root beer, I get it," I yelled.

"Why does he get it?" whined bouncing Fred.

Mom grabbed each of us by an arm and gave a stiff shake.

"You two settle down before your father gets upset. You know he doesn't like it when you behave like hooligans in public."

Putting my shoulder back into its socket, I glanced ahead to see if Dad had heard the commotion. I saw a pink stain all over the seat of his gray slacks. Fred saw it too, and immediately his mouth was activated.

"Hey, Dad, how come you got a pink butt?"

I thought Mom was going to faint. Dad turned on her like a wounded grizzly, a puzzled scowl covering his face.

"What's he talking about?"

Mom tried to appear unconcerned.

"Well, dear, it looks like you were sweating back there, and the seat cover stained your pants a little. I didn't even notice it myself."

"It's great big," said Fred.

Dad tried to see the stain by looking over his shoulder, then by sticking his head under one arm and turning in circles. Finally he thought to back up to the side mirror on the Buick. Viewing the extent of the pink reflection, he let loose an amazing string of profane words. I had heard most of them before, but a few of the longer ones were rather ambiguous.

"Johnathon Kane!" Mom said, looking around to see if anyone else was near enough to have heard.

Droplets of sweat slid down Dad's temples. "So what's a guy supposed to do? I got such wonderful luck. I drive over a hundred and fifty miles, all I want is a beer, and I can't even go inside because my stinking pants are pink. That's enough to make the Pope cuss."

"Don't worry about your clothes, Dad," said Fred cheerily, "just walk in the joint and feel good about it."

Two minutes later we were on the road again, substantially exceeding the sixty miles per hour limit. Dad yelled at slow drivers, Mom chewed an aspirin, and Fred slumped to the floor behind the front seat, dribbling tears on his shirt, whining how mean everyone was to keep him from using the restroom or getting some pop. I was content to sit and imagine the Pope, speaking to adoring throngs at the Vatican, hurling cuss words at them like a Saturday night drunkard. Such a thought was hilarious, but I didn't dare laugh.

On the outskirts of the next town we stopped at a gas station with a playful-looking green dinosaur on the sign. We drove over a thin, black hose, and a bell rang. A pimple-faced attendant strolled out of the garage.

"Whut kin ah do for you-all?"

"Fill it with regular," Dad said.

"You bet."

Mom and Fred ran to the restrooms. Dad waited for the attendant to start pumping gas; then he went to the trunk, pulling a pair of pants from a suitcase.

"Say, whereabouts you-all headed for?" asked the pimple-faced guy.

"All the way to the promised land," Dad said, backing away.

The guy's eyes got big. "Californy? Man, ah'd give ever'thing ah got to go to Californy."

Dad looked like he wanted to laugh in the guy's face, but doubtless it was difficult to be too arrogant while a pink splotch covered the seat of his pants. "We're only going to Sedalia, so don't get too excited. I'm going to use your toilet for a minute."

"You bet."

The attendant took a rag from his pocket and jammed it under the trigger on the pump handle so he could leave to run a chamois over our bug-splattered windshield.

"You-all got kin down there in Sedaly?" he asked me.

"Nah, we're just visiting some relatives."

He shrugged and continued removing insect remains. Mom and Fred returned to the car.

"I don't think that floor has seen a mop in months," Mom said, opening her purse. "It smelled like a barn."

"Ah reckon that's my fault, ma'am. Ah'm supposed to keep things lookin' good 'round here, but ah get a little scaredy when it comes to steppin' foot inside the ladies' facility."

I knew by the embarrassed look on Mom's face that she was afraid the guy had been offended. She was not the type who enjoyed making people feel small.

"Well, that's perfectly understandable. Actually, it wasn't that bad at all. Maybe it just needed to be aired out a little."

"You said it smelled like somebody peed in every corner," Fred reminded her.

Luckily for Mom's peace of mind, the attendant had moved away from us to check on the gas. After shooing Fred into the backseat, she handed me four dimes for the red Coke machine just outside the station door. When I came back balancing four frosted bottles, Dad was getting into the Buick and the guy was peering at the numbers on the pump.

"What's the damage?" Dad asked him.

"Looks like 'bout three dollars 'n fifty two cents for the gas, 'n then ah'm gonna have to charge you-all two cents apiece for them bottles. Let's see now, four two's is eight, 'n eight hooked onta three fifty-two 'd be, uh, carry the one—"

"Three-sixty," Dad said through clenched teeth. "Here's a five, ace. That should cover it."

"You bet."

While the attendant went into the station for change, Fred and I gulped our Cokes. Mom held the other two as Dad studied the map.

"Missouri is twelve miles away," he said.

Mom put one of the bottles to his lips. "Little sip?" He nodded, and she tipped the Coke for him. Some of the brown liquid went into his mouth, some ran down onto his shirt.

"Watch out, woman, you're pouring it all over me!"

Mom pulled the bottle back, dabbing at his chest with a tissue. "Sorry, dear."

"Well I should hope so. I just get my pants changed and now I need another shirt. I'll probably be wearing a straitjacket before it's all said and done."

Fred leaned over the seat. "Guess what, Mom. I know just what Dad should have worn today."

"What's that, Freddy?"

"Pink pants and brown shirt . . . Then nobody could see all the spots."

His remark was so stupid that I couldn't help laughing. Some of the Coke bubbled out of my nose. Dad turned around and gave us a stare that lowered the backseat temperature thirty degrees. Fred slid down into a spineless heap, sucking on the neck of his pop bottle. I wiped my nose on my sleeve.

"Got yore change, sir. You-all have a safe trip now, hear?"

The attendant handed Dad several bills plus some coins. For a second there was silence inside the car. Mom started to protest, but Dad jerked the transmission into gear and we shot out of the driveway, leaving the pimple-faced guy waving behind us.

"There's too much money here," Mom said. "I think he gave us change for a twenty-dollar bill."

"Good for us, bad for him," Dad said. "Gimme that Coke."

"Johnathon, this isn't right. A thing like that could cost that young man his job. I want you to turn this car around right now."

With one long pull on the bottle, Dad reduced the contents by half, then threw the rest out the window. "That stuff won't ever replace Schlitz, I'll tell you that."

Mom glowered at him a long time, then turned away. The next twelve miles were silent except for the tires thumping over cracks in the blacktop. Then we passed a sign welcoming us to the "show me" state.

"We're in Missouri, men," Dad said.

Fred sat up. "Where?"

"All around us."

"How come it looks just like Iowa did?"

Dad chose not to answer Fred, the same way he chose not to answer Mom about the money. His was certainly an effective way of cutting short a conversation or ducking a tough question, but he was the only one allowed to practice such a thing. Rank did indeed have its privileges.

As the miles rolled by, boredom combined with heat to induce a sleep lasting until early evening. When I awoke, my stomach told me it was open for business. We hadn't eaten anything since breakfast, except some oatmeal cookies Mom brought along.

The air rushing past the windows was slightly cooler now, just enough to make a person feel human again. When the sun's decline was in its final half-hour, Dad spotted a sign saying Sedalia was two miles away.

"That's the one we've been waiting for," he said, erupting into a minor explosion of off-key whistling.

The whistling made me wonder if it might be safe to ask a question. I took the chance.

"Which one of our relatives lives here?"

"Your Grandfather Kane has a place of business here," Mom said.

Grandfather Kane? I vaguely recalled an old man visiting us years ago, when I was in kindergarten. I attended school half-days, and when I came home he would be waiting on the porch for me. All I remembered of him was his breath; it always smelled like some cheap mouthwash. Maybe he ate a lot of onions.

The blacktop we had been following since the dawn of creation widened as we approached the city. It divided and rejoined at irregular intervals, picking up more traffic at each junction with a lesser road. Numerous signs made it difficult to concentrate on driving for fear of missing important directions. In the time it took to read one sign, two others were overlooked. Dad was no longer whistling.

"It's like driving in a stampede," he complained as cars pressed closely on all sides of the Buick. "They build a new road and a guy has to be Einstein to find a place he's known all his life. Stinking world."

"I can't understand why there's so much traffic tonight," Mom said.

"The rodeo must be in town this week. That figures."

By now the other vehicles had their lights on. We moved cautiously among a galaxy of yellow circles as darkness began seeping through the windows. Fred rubbed his sleep-encrusted eyes. "Aren't we ever going to be there?" he moaned.

"Shut your whining mouth," Dad ordered.

"Just a few more minutes, honey," Mom said.

A car came at us with its brights on. Dad put a hand to his eyes. "Dim it, you idiot or . . . Hey, what did that sign say?"

"I wasn't looking, dear," Mom said.

"Well, wake up. I only got one set of eyes, you know. A guy drives four hundred miles and his family won't even help him look for signs."

Mom sighed. "I guess we're all a little tired."

"Yeah, reading them women's magazines is really tough."

After some minor miscalculations and one U-turn, we turned into the driveway of a shabby-looking gas station. Two ancient pumps stood out front; a flashing red sign above the front door promised Budweiser to whomever might seek it.

"Thank God we're here," Mom said.

"Thank me," Dad said, "I did the driving."

Something wasn't right about the place. The outside lights

were off, except for a small security bulb, and nobody came out to wait on us.

"I don't think they're open," I said.

"We're not here to get gas, Tommy," Mom explained. "This is your Grandfather Kane's place."

"He lives in a gas station?"

"There are rooms in back. You'll see in a minute."

After we got out of the car, Dad smoothed his clothes and combed his hair. Mom put on fresh lipstick, then checked her children for dangling shirttails. They acted nervous, like whenever the landlord stopped by to see how we were treating his property. Cars were zooming by. Bugs flying around the security light had discovered our presence and were telling all their friends.

"Let's get inside," Dad said, pushing us ahead of him toward the door.

I was ready to knock when Fred turned the knob and walked right in as if he had lived there all his life. We followed. In seconds the overpowering stench of beer and cigarette smoke found its way up my nose. What kind of gas station was this supposed to be? Rather than stacks of oil cans or antifreeze, as one might expect, I saw an L-shaped bar dominating two sides of the room. Several booths lined another wall. There was also a pinball machine and a jukebox. Either this was one of Dad's dumb jokes or we were in the wrong place.

A woman with dark hair drawn tightly back against her head was wiping off the bar. Her face looked like it belonged on an Indian squaw. She had orange-colored lips and dark, slanted eyes and wore a red and white checked dress that might have once been a tablecloth. "They're here," she yelled into a back room that was separated from the bar area by a yellow blanket hung over the doorway. A tired-looking little man pushed his way past the flimsy divider.

"There's a sight for my old eyes," he said, moving around the woman and emerging from behind the bar, arms outstretched. He got to Mom first, giving her a hug and a kiss on the cheek. "Hello, Louise, you cute little heifer."

Fred turned to me. "Did he cuss?"

"Shut up."

Grandpa Kane wore a light-blue sport shirt, somewhat wrinkled, made of a material so transparent that I could see the straps on his undershirt as he bent over to squeeze Fred's neck. "Who's this little boogernose?" he asked.

"I'm Fred."

"Well, how ya doin' there, Mr. Fred?"

"I got to use the toilet real bad."

The old man laughed hoarsely and told the woman to show Fred where to go. He called her Ruth.

As Fred walked stiff-legged around the bar, I happened to glance at Dad. His face was flushed, and his eyes looked strange. I assumed he was embarrassed because of what Fred had just said.

"Don't tell me this is old Tommy Toughstuff," Grandpa said, grabbing my hand.

"Guess so."

Pulling me toward him, he made an awkward attempt at a hug. I noticed he was shorter than me. The stubble on his cheek felt like bristles on a hairbrush as it grazed my neck. His breath still hung in the air, like years before, but I realized now it was not mouthwash that caused the odor. It was whiskey. We held close for several seconds, then he stiffened. I stepped back and saw he was looking at Dad. Grandpa's thin gray hair was slicked against his head, making the large ears look even more oversized. His eyes were more red than blue.

"Good to see ya, Junior," he said.

Dad mumbled something I couldn't hear, then they embraced. Nobody seemed to know what to do while the two men held on to each other. Mom sat on one of the bar stools, twisting back and forth. Ruth needlessly ran a rag along the top of the bar. The only sounds came from a small, rotating fan, and from Fred flushing the toilet somewhere in back.

When they finally separated, Grandpa pulled a wrinkled handkerchief from his pocket and wiped his nose. Something fell to the floor between him and Dad, making a small spot on the scuffed, brown wood. A second spot appeared and then a third. They were Dad's tears. He was trying to hold his emotions inside, but a loud sob escaped and filled the room. I had never heard him cry before. A boy grows up hearing his father talking and laughing and yelling, seldom thinking twice about such things. But to hear him cry is something not soon forgotten.

"Grandpa gots a big bird back there," announced Fred, punching his way past the yellow blanket. "It's green."

The embarrassment of the previous moment faded as Grandpa went behind the divider and came back carrying a parrot for us to admire. While Ruth opened frosted bottles of pop and beer, he informed us that the bird's name was Stan the Man, in honor of St. Louis Cardinal legend Stan Musial. We watched with delight as it ate kernels of popcorn from our hands and waddled the length and width of the bar searching for other edibles. Occasionally the bird said its name or said "pretty baby" or cussed. We liked it best when he cussed.

When the novelty of a foul-mouthed fowl wore off, I slipped away from the chattering crowd to take a closer look at my Grandpa Kane's surroundings. Carrying the remainder of my soda, an unusual and totally unfamiliar drink called Dr. Pepper, I crossed into the unseen area behind the yellow blanket. The living quarters consisted of three tiny rooms, sparsely furnished, plus a bath. The bedroom had separate beds against opposite walls with just enough space in between for walking. The kitchen wasn't much bigger than the stove, and the third room contained only a worn sofa and a small television with dimestore rabbit ears on top.

Back out in the barroom the atmosphere was pure tavern. The air was full of smoke and loud conversation. Beer bottles cluttered the booth where Grandpa sat with my family. I felt no inclination to become part of the group, choosing instead to sit at the bar and observe all the beer paraphernalia covering the shelves along the back wall. Budweiser, Schlitz, and Miller had their names on everything from ashtrays to lampshades.

All those items, brightly-colored and gaudy, contrasted with the drab decorum on the far side of the yellow blanket. They seemed to indicate that whatever excitement or happiness existed inside this place would be found in the barroom. A sadness was growing behind the blanket, an emptiness, like the one lurking inside my own body, only older and more powerful. Out in the barroom, people laughed and listened to music and told funny stories; behind the blanket, wallpaper patterns were memorized while hands on the clock ran an endless circular track to eternity.

But I knew from experience that all of this was a lie, an illusion. The happiness of a drunk is as temporary as the sensation of flight one feels after jumping off a roof. The momentary release from the forces pulling against us is seldom worth the inevitable crash-landing that follows. I had seen too many drunks in too many places to believe that drinking was a method of attaining anything worthwhile. Perhaps true happiness was a myth, like Heaven; but if it did exist somewhere, the pathway leading to it would certainly not be strewn with empty bottles.

I rotated on the red bar stool to look at the people in the booth. Grandpa Kane sat opposite my parents, while Fred hopped back and forth like a politician. Ruth stood off to one side, never taking part in the conversation or interacting in any way with Mom or Dad. The frozen smile upon her face seemed unreal. I remembered we had not been introduced to her.

Before I could dwell on that little mystery any further, Grandpa proposed a toast. Everyone at the table lifted a bottle.

"To my son and his family. I've missed 'em bad."

The bottles had no sooner clinked together when Dad broke down again. Grandpa started crying too. I knew I had to get out of there for a while. The combined effects of a long trip, thickening smoke, and rampant emotion had finally taken their toll. I needed space and fresh air. As the others wiped away their tears, I slipped out the back door. Half an hour passed before anyone came looking.

• • • •

Grandpa Kane was the one who found me sitting on a tree stump, enjoying the Missouri night breeze. He carried a flashlight and a small paper bag. Occasional forks of heat lightning jabbed the darkened horizon.

"You like explodin' crackers?" he asked.

"Never ate one."

"Ya don't eat 'em, ya monkey. Ya stick a match to 'em."

"Are you talking about firecrackers?"

"What yuh think? Here . . . let's use some of these up. I got tons." He reached into the bag, pulling out a handful of Black Beauties. "Gimme your lighter."

"I don't have a lighter," I told him.

"You better not! Smokin' ruins a man's health."

"Don't you smoke?"

"Course I do. How ya think I got my health ruined? Now hold this."

He gave me one of the firecrackers, then took out his own cigarette lighter from a shirt pocket. When flame touched fuse and sparks began to fly, I made a quick toss.

"Bombs over Tokyo!" Grandpa yelled.

The firecracker hit the grass and fizzled. We waited several seconds to avoid becoming victims of a slow burn. Nothing happened. Tokyo was spared.

"A dud," I said.

"Maybe not. Dew on the grass might have killed the flame. Hold on to the next one."

"Hold on to it?"

"You betcha. Just light up an' let 'er blow."

I assumed he was just being silly. Holding on to an exploding firecracker was an experience I had accidentally endured while showing off for my friends the previous Summer. My right hand carried the scars. The last thing I needed was a matching set.

"You show me how it's done," I said.

In the moonlight I saw a smile cross his seamed face. He handed me the flashlight and lighter, grabbed a firecracker, and held it at the very end between his thumb and index finger.

"Light me."

I did as he ordered. Grandpa kept smiling as he extended his arm away from his body. I took three steps backwards. Despite his confident manner, I expected him to throw off at the last minute. Then came the startling flash and the crack of detonation.

"Wow," I yelled in spite of myself. "Are you hurt?"

The smile was gone. "Yes, I am."

I grabbed at his small, veined hand, shining the flashlight upon it. Nothing appeared to be damaged.

"Where at?"

He put the hand on my shoulder. "I'm hurting in places you can't see."

"Why?"

"Well, maybe it's because I got a grandson I ain't seen for years who's actin' like he don't want no part of me. He'd rather sit out here talkin' to the weeds instead of bein' where I'm at."

Katydids whined incessantly from nearby trees. I could hear music coming from the jukebox inside as the Everly Brothers implored Little Susie to wake up. Grandpa's breath was stronger than ever.

"Sorry," I said. "It wasn't anything against you. It's just been a crazy day. I needed some air."

He coughed, then sniffled. "Aw, don't pay no attention to me. I get feelin' sorry for myself sometimes, that's all. Whatsay we get back inside before that little boogernose Fred drinks all the Dr. Pepper."

"What about the firecrackers?"

"We'll shoot 'em off another day. We got time ahead of us."

I followed him back inside the gas station, where conditions had deteriorated. A fog of cigarette smoke had formed. Dad held yet another beer in his hand; his face was telltale red. Fred was playing the pinball machine; the flashing lights and clanging bells evoked a twinge of pain between my eyes. Ruth smiled at me as she poured a bottle of pop over ice pellets inside a Michelob glass. Mom was somewhere behind the yellow blanket.

Dad looked up from his beer. "Where you been?"

"Outside," I answered.

"I know that, dummy. I meant, what were you doing out there?"

Before I could respond, Grandpa pointed a finger in Dad's direction. "The kid was just gettin' some air, Junior, so shut yer face an' let him be. Here, Tommy, here's a quarter. Play some of that roller rock on the jukebox. That stuff makes my feet jump around."

I expected Dad to throw a fit after being told to shut up, but he only shrugged. Was he still scared of his father in some small way? Does a son spend his entire life under his father's thumb? I didn't plan to. When I became a man, Dad would give me respect or end up on his back. He would never again call me "dummy" or treat me like small change. I would fear him no more.

Two more hours passed before we finally left the gas station or tavern or whatever it was. Mom called ahead to reserve a room at a nearby motel. We were fortunate that traffic had nearly vanished by the time we took to the road, because Dad kept steering the Buick across the center line. To compensate, he jerked the wheel in the opposite direction, causing Mom to scream about him running us into the ditch. Dad got mad and yelled that maybe she wanted to drive. At that point I would rather have taken my chances with the rookie.

The Night Shade Motel wasn't much to look at, but it had showers and air conditioning. We took full advantage of both. Fred fell asleep as soon as his body touched the clean sheets. Mom got Dad to lay down "for a second," knowing he would not get back up. I spent half an hour in the shower letting cold water lower my body temperature. By the time I left the bathroom, everybody else was asleep. I rolled Fred away from the air conditioner, then lay down directly in the middle of the frigid breeze. Sleep was immediate.

Just past 3 I awoke after having a strange dream. It had something to do with me tossing firecrackers at Jimmy Swailes, then seeing him lying in the street. My hands were scarred and blood-covered. I ran into a nearby gas station, where Carlos Montez poured me a glass of strawberry pop. He wore a red and white checked shirt and was smiling an evil smile.

Despite the cool room, my dream caused me to wake up sweating. I stared into the darkness, listening to Dad snore. It sounded like excavating equipment was moving earth beneath the floor. To take my mind off the bizarre dream and the noise, I made a mental list of baseball's greatest home run hitters. I got as far as Lou Gehrig with 493, then my brain took the rest of the night off.

MISSOURI

We were out of the hotel by 9 o'clock, eating breakfast at a place next door called Louie's Bacon 'n Egg Heaven. I hadn't gotten enough sleep and was hating the whole world, especially the cook who fried my bacon in motor oil. The strips were so slippery that I could barely keep them on my plate.

Considering that Dad should have been tired and hungover, his disposition bordered on the miraculous. Instead of his usual surly self, he was soft-spoken and patient. When I dripped runny, yellow egg yolk on my clean shirt, he merely winked and offered me a dampened napkin. Even more amazing was his reaction when Fred tried to eat a piece of toast after fumbling it under the table.

"We don't eat things after they've been on the floor, son," he said calmly.

Fred's mouth and eyes opened to their maximum. "Boy, Tommy, ain't Dad being nice to us today?"

Dad only shrugged, as if he couldn't understand why anyone should be surprised at his good behavior.

Soon we were back on the road. The temperature wasn't as high as the day before, but the car was just as crowded with junk and my rear was just as sore from riding. I assumed we would head back to Grandpa Kane's place, but Dad turned us in the opposite direction, onto a disintegrating blacktop highway.

"Where we going?" I asked Mom.

"We're on the road to Climer."

"What's that?"

"It's where the rest of your father's relatives live, and where he lived for a while when he was a boy."

I was curious to know why we had never heard anything about these relatives before now, but such a question might put Dad in a bad mood.

After nearly half an hour of being shaken and bounced, like on some cheap carnival ride, we exited onto a narrow gravel road. A weathered sign told us Climer was four miles ahead.

"We're so close now I can almost smell it," Dad said.

"Me too," Fred said.

A set of railroad tracks angled toward us from a distant bluff, eventually paralleling the road.

"We used to walk those tracks when we were kids," Dad told Mom.

I couldn't imagine my dad being a kid or walking on railroad tracks. I tried, but it just wouldn't register. Watching him absorb the sight of familiar scenery, I sensed he was feeling good. More than that, he seemed at peace with the world. I couldn't remember ever seeing him that way before. Curiously, it made me feel good too.

The Buick picked up speed as we neared our final destination. Maybe it was unintentional, or maybe Dad was getting anxious, but we left a dust cloud behind us resembling a London fog. Rocks bounced off the undercarriage of the car as if we were being machine-gunned. Mom's hand squeezed the armrest on the door. Then came a rickety wooden bridge that looked like it had been built with horses in mind. Tired planking rattled a vigorous protest as the Buick shot across it at twice the recommended speed.

A small but steep hill slowed us considerably; the speedometer dropped below 45. Mom's facial color returned. One last bend in the road took us through a grove of towering oaks. When we emerged again into sunlight, there was a town resting just beyond our front bumper.

"Main Street," Dad said softly.

I stared at the collection of buildings in front of me and felt sick. It was hardly even a town. Main Street was little more than two blocks long. Its ugly orange brick structures leaned against one another like some of Dad's buddies after a long night of drinking.

For this we had come five hundred miles? It made McKinley look like Chicago.

Halfway into town, or halfway out, we turned onto a short dead end called Second Street. I knew the name from a hand-painted sign nailed to a tree near the corner. Dad drove the Buick down the driveway of a three-storied white house, the only build-ing on that side of the street. He honked the horn as we piled out of the car. The back door of the house opened. Two gray-haired ladies, bespectacled and wearing dresses that looked hopelessly out of any recent style, came waddling toward us.

"Junior, it is so good to have you back," said the shorter, heavier one, wrapping her arms around Dad's waist and bear-hugging him. The other lady embraced Mom. I wondered why everyone in Missouri insisted on calling Dad "Junior." I had never heard any-one else call him that before, although he accepted it without com-ment.

When they were finished with our parents, the ladies came after Fred and me. After an awesome display of hugging and squeezing, the perfume they wore took away whatever breath remained in our lungs. They commented how handsome and intel-ligent we both looked. I was mature enough not to let such flattery affect me, but Fred got carried away. He made the old ladies watch while he attempted a cartwheel. Somehow he ended up rolling into a thorny rosebush, and they made a big fuss over his phony cries of pain. He was promised a dish of homemade ice cream when we got inside. Being an idiot was not without its advantages.

We entered the house through a small porch that was cluttered with potted plants and wicker furniture. Mom told me that the old ladies, introduced as Aunt Julia and Aunt Inez, were Grandpa Kane's sisters. I really didn't care too much about who they were; old women made me nervous, especially the kind who liked to hug.

"Let's go into the dining room," said Julia, the short, plump one. Her heels made rapid clicking sounds against the polished wood floors as she led us through a kitchen and down a long hall-way. The wallpaper in the hall was patterned with bright yellow tulips. We turned into a large dining room with a glass chandelier hanging from a high ceiling. A woman waited there, hands on hips.

"C'mere, you two," Dad said to Fred and me. "This is your second cousin Belle. She's Aunt Inez's daughter."

"Well now," said the woman in a husky voice that oozed arrogance, "another generation of Kanes has come back to Climer. What do you think of our little village?"

"I like it a lot," Fred said.

Belle laughed. Her lips, colored reddish-purple by lipstick, pulled away from straight but slightly yellow teeth. Her black hair looked stiff. She wore an expensive-looking chartreuse dress with a low neckline. Turquoise jewelry decorated her hands and wrists. Her confident expression hinted that she was used to having her own way. I had already decided not to give her the time of day.

"Ain't much of a town," I said with exaggerated indifference.

Again she laughed, putting a hand on my forearm. Despite the heat, her touch was cool. The nails of her fingers were colored the same reddish-purple shade as her lips.

"At last an honest man has come to this house," she said. "I think we'll get along famously."

"There now," said Julia, "we've all been introduced, and it's time for the ice cream we promised little Freddy. I'll get bowls for everybody."

"I don't think I want any, Julia," Dad said. "You go ahead while I start taking stuff out of the car."

"But it's peach, Junior. That was always your favorite."

Dad was halfway to the hall. "Thanks anyway."

"All right then, but Poppa will be very disappointed if you don't have some. He made it himself, you know."

Dad stopped. "The Chief made it?"

"Just this morning. He's freshening up and should be coming downstairs anytime now."

"Well, maybe I'd better have a little. No sense getting him upset."

He sheepishly took a seat with the rest of us around a long, wooden dining table. Belle had an amused expression upon her face; Julia appeared much relieved. I couldn't help but be curious at all the commotion over a dish of ice cream. Who was the Chief, and why was he capable of making Dad so nervous?

The aunts served ice cream in delicate white bowls with small, blue flowers painted on the outside. I knew nothing about dishes, but it didn't take too many brains to figure out that if one of these bowls was broken, a duplicate would not be found at the nearest dime store. The ice cream itself was absolutely the best I had ever tasted. It was creamy, unbelievably cold, and full of delicious bits of peach pulp. I was well into my second helping when an old man walked into the room. He leaned on a polished hickory cane. There was an instant change in the atmosphere, much like when a school principal enters a classroom.

"We're all enjoying the ice cream, Poppa," Inez said, jumping from her seat to pull out a chair for the old man.

He waved her away with a flick of his veined wrist. "Sit, sit. All I want to do is say hello to the Iowa branch of the Kane clan. Get over here, Junior."

Dad almost ran to shake the old man's hand; Mom did the same. Fred and I gulped down what remained in our bowls, fearing it would melt while we endured another introduction. Between mouthfuls I watched the old man as he talked to my parents. He looked to be just under six feet tall, and solid for someone of his years. His hair was completely white, and so was the bushy mustache covering his upper lip. Despite the heat, he wore a long-sleeved gray shirt and heavy, baggy pants with black suspenders.

Dad was in the middle of some story when the old man cut him off. "Let's meet your boys."

"Oh, sure thing . . . Kids, this is your great-grandfather Oliver Spencer Kane, better known in this part of the state as 'Chief.' He used to be the county fire chief years back, and—"

"Spare us the ancient history lesson," ordered the Chief, "my mouth still works fine."

"Yes, sir," Dad mumbled.

I stood up and shook the man's hand.

"You're Thomas Jamison, aren't you," he said.

I was embarrassed to hear my middle name mentioned in public. Of the many things I didn't like about myself, that name was at the top of the list.

"Yeah, that's me," I said.

His cold blue eyes looked straight into mine.

"Say 'yes, sir,' not 'yeah' when you speak," he commanded.

His order caught me off-guard. "Yes, sir!"

"That is better, Thomas Jamison. You must realize that Jamison was your great-grandmother's maiden name, and a darn good name it is. Be proud of it."

"Yes, sir." Now I knew why people got nervous when this guy walked into a room. He was something else!

"You must be Fredric," the Chief said to my brother, "but I don't recall your middle name."

"Allen."

"Yes . . . Allen. I don't know that we've ever had any Allens in the family before. Nothing wrong with that name, although there are others that might have been better."

"Can I have some more ice cream?" blurted Fred, obviously not interested in a discussion of middle names.

The Chief stiffened. "We're not through talking yet, young man."

"I am," said Fred.

Everyone laughed uneasily, except for the old man. Ignoring the remark, he sat down at the table and began firing questions at Dad. He wanted to know about the trip down from Iowa, the economic situation in McKinley, gas mileage for the Buick, and other equally boring subjects. Occasionally he spoke to me. I answered as best I could, remembering to say "yes, sir," and tried to avoid prolonged contact with those probing eyes. Not another word was spoken to Fred. I wasn't sure if the Chief thought my brother had too smart a mouth, or if he just didn't like talking to someone whose middle name was Allen.

Nearly an hour passed before we left the table to begin unpacking the car. Dad wanted to get everything inside with one trip, so we loaded ourselves down like cargo-bearing slaves. I had a suitcase in each hand and a clothes bag draped over my shoulder.

"I still can't believe we brought all this junk," panted Dad, staggering across the kitchen.

"By the time we get it upstairs, you'll be a believer," Mom said.

"Real funny, woman."

Once again we passed through the hallway of yellow tulips, turning opposite of the dining room toward a steep wall of red-carpeted stairs.

The second floor of the Kane home was like nothing I had seen before. It consisted of seven bedrooms, each with a brass number upon the door. Every room contained a marble-topped vanity, a chest of drawers, and a brass bed sitting high off the floor.

"This place sure has enough bedrooms," I said to Mom.

"That's because it used to be a hotel. The Chief ran it until 1949 or so."

"1948," said Dad, dropping his suitcases in the doorway of bedroom number 5.

"Yes, I guess it was. Tommy was just a baby when we were here."

"I've been here before?"

"For a couple of months. We stayed here when your great-grandmother Eleanor, the Chief's wife, took sick. Your father worked on a construction crew in Sedalia. We almost bought a little house on the edge of town."

"So how come you didn't?"

Dad reached out and grabbed me by the arm. "That's none of your business. Get down to number 6 and start unpacking. I don't know why you have to play twenty questions every time there's work to get done."

I jerked away. Mom saw that I was about to say something back to him. She put a finger to her lips and motioned with her head for me to move along. I obeyed her, but inside I was ready to explode. How was I supposed to deal with Dad's crazy moods? One minute he was patient and friendly, the next he was irate because I asked a simple question. The man was impossible to live with.

I dragged the two suitcases across the threshold of room number 6. Fred was already jamming his clothes into the chest of drawers. A minute later Julia entered the room.

"Are we getting all settled in?" she asked, setting a maroon vase of flowers on the vanity.

"Yes, ma'am." I didn't mind showing manners to her; she seemed nice, even if she was an old lady.

After arranging the flowers to suit her, Julia gave Fred a monstrous hug. "Oh, it's so nice having young hearts inside this place again. I'm afraid we've all grown old around here, and we need a shot of new blood to perk us up." She released Fred and came at me. I braced myself for the same treatment, but she only cupped my chin in her hand. "You remind me of your grandfather when he was a boy, Sugar. I'm busy right now, but after dinner we'll get out the picture albums and you'll see what I mean."

Fred shadowed her downstairs, asking about more ice cream. Mom and Dad soon followed. I was glad for the opportunity to be alone. Being called "Sugar" had made me think of Jimmy. He often played upon my last name by calling me "Candy Kane" or "Sugar Kane." Had it only been a week since his death? So much had happened, it felt like a year. I wondered what was going on back home. Had the furor over the house painting died down? I hoped it was still a hot issue, and that Hippo would think up something else to fan the flames during my absence. Five hundred miles was not enough distance to separate me from my hatred of Carlos Montez. I still wanted him to pay dearly for the sight of a young boy lying bloody in the street. No power on earth could change my feelings about that!

I flopped down on the high brass bed, enjoying the solitude. As had become my habit lately, I took a look at the inscription inside Jimmy's ring. "I am the way, the truth, and the life" wasn't particularly hard to remember, but I still had no idea what it meant. Oddly enough, the simple act of reading that phrase had a soothing effect upon me. It made no sense that nine words inside a cheap ring could do such a thing, but it happened every time.

Another feeling came over me as I lay upon the bed. I suddenly believed myself to be on the edge of some wonderful discovery, some life-changing event. Only a fool would expect to find anything in Climer, Missouri other than boredom; yet deep inside my being, amid the swirling emotions of a normal thirteen-year-old, something unfamiliar seemed to be awakening. I couldn't explain it any more than I could explain the mysterious empty spot living within me. All I knew for sure was that having so many strange, new things taking root inside me had made it rather crowded down there. Something would eventually have to give.

MISSOURI

*T*he most beautiful spot in the hotel was the parlor. Just off the backside of the kitchen was a short hallway leading to that room. Visitors entered the parlor through French doors that were adorned with glass knobs resembling huge, multifaceted diamonds. Once inside they would see a Steinway piano, four high-backed wooden chairs with crimson padding, and a delicate love seat that matched the chairs. In the corner opposite the piano sat a cabinet full of fragile-looking glass animals of every imaginable variety and color. A portrait of Eleanor Kane, the Chief's deceased wife, dominated one wall, and large windows with leaded glass took up most of two others. The room had an aura of mystery about it that only intensified when Fred and I were informed we could never enter there unless invited by an adult. As of the third day, no invitation had been extended.

The Sunday morning after our arrival I stood, hands in pockets and brain in limbo, peering through the glass which separated me from that wonderful room. My thoughts were interrupted by the sound of someone entering the kitchen through the back-porch door.

"Anybody awake 'round this joint?" asked a familiar voice. I walked down the short hallway to the kitchen and saw Grandpa Kane. "Well, if it ain't the firecracker kid," he said. "I brought the sack with me so we can finish off what we started the other night. You interested?"

"Sure, but Dad just told me to stay inside because we're going away pretty soon."

"It's Grandpa!" yelled Fred as he came into the kitchen carrying a dirty plate.

"Shhh," whispered Grandpa, "the old man might still be around here someplace."

"If you mean the Chief," I said, "he left already."

The cautious manner evaporated. "Good," he said. "I figured he'd be gone by now, but that ol' buzzard likes to mess me up when he gets the chance. Where's your dad at?"

"He's eating," Fred said.

"Well, I'm gonna talk at him a minute, then we're gonna go to a carnival. How ya like that, Boogernose?"

"Oh boy," squealed Fred, "We ain't been to a carnival since we was little kids."

Grandpa winked at me and jauntily stepped in the direction of the dining room. When Mom and Dad looked up from their plates of scrambled eggs and saw him, their mouths forgot to keep chewing.

Belle sat in a green overstuffed chair painting her nails. She flashed him a cynical smile. "While the cat's away the rat will play?"

Grandpa threw up his hands in mock surrender. "You're gonna have to spend a little longer on your makeup, Bellebutton—your ugly side is showin' through this morning."

Belle clenched her jaw, reddening slightly, but said nothing. I got the impression she was overmatched, and my opinion of Grandpa Kane rose considerably.

Inez came down the stairs into the dining room. She, too, acted shocked to see her brother. "Good heavens, is Poppa still in the hotel?"

"He's out squirtin' the fires of Hell," said Grandpa.

Inez fanned herself with her hand. "That's a relief. We don't need any fireworks on a Sunday morning!"

"Well now, old girl, fireworks is one of the reasons I'm here. I got this bag full of crackers that need to be shot up before the day's over, an' since you don't seem too interested I thought I'd give 'em to the boys. An' since it's the last day for the carnival over at Hadleyville, I thought we'd go over there a while. What yuh think, Junior?"

All eyes turned to Dad, who hadn't touched his food since Grandpa came into the room. "Boy oh boy, uh, I just don't know," he stammered.

"Please, Dad," begged Fred. "We'll be good."

"Live dangerous, Junior," Belle smirked.

"Well, it's just that I sort of told the Chief I'd go to church this morning."

"Did ya tell him ya'd bring the boys?" Grandpa asked.

"I didn't exactly say it, but I know he's expecting them."

Grandpa walked over to the table and stuck his face close to Dad's. "Do these guys go to church any other time?"

"Not too often," Dad mumbled.

"I ain't never been to church," Fred said.

Grandpa shook his head. "That's what I figured! Junior, you ain't nothin' but a snivelin' hypocrite if ya make 'em go there today instead of doin' something fun like a carnival."

I waited for Dad to explode at such an accusation, but it never happened. He just sat there sweating. "But what will I tell the Chief?"

"Just tell him that the biggest sinner in the world added another rock to his pile. I don't see how takin' two boys to a carnival is wrong, but he'll make it seem like a hangin' offense, so just let him blame me for everything an' you'll be in the clear. See you people later. Let's roll, boys."

Inez stood in the middle of the room looking helpless. "Brother, I don't think Poppa is going to approve of this."

Grandpa gave her a passing peck on the cheek. "If he ever approved of something I did, the sky would fall down. Keep yer powder dry, little sister."

The hall clock struck 9:30 as Fred and I followed Grandpa toward the front door. I made a quick detour upstairs to get my billfold. It contained thirty-eight dollars, the sum total of savings accumulated by Fred and me over recent years. Only thirty-three of it was mine, but I carried the whole wad because Fred had a habit of losing things from his pockets.

Grandpa's car, a blue '57 Chevy wagon, was full of dust and trash. The front seat was reasonably free of debris, but the rear area was littered with everything from empty beer cans to lawn chairs to broken flowerpots with bits of dead plants still clinging to the dirt. As we drove down Main Street, the entire collection of junk shook, rattled, and rolled, but Grandpa didn't notice—or didn't care.

"We sure showed them guys how it's done, didn't we," he laughed, poking a finger in my ribs.

"Yeah, we did," I said, "but won't the Chief be mad?"

"Course he will. He'll get so worked up that he'll have to sit down an' read Revelation or Deuteronomy a couple times just to cool off."

"What's dooderominee?" asked Fred.

"Oh, it's a special mixture they serve up in church. It's made from sugar an' horse manure."

"Yuck!" said Fred. "I'm glad we ain't going to church."

"Now yer talkin', Boogernose."

Just ahead of us, a rabbit darted onto the road. Grandpa swerved the car to avoid hitting it. "Look out there, ol' jackrabbit, else I'll make a stick of gum outta ya."

Fred giggled. "This is fun, Grandpa. I'm glad we're with you instead of our dad."

The old man's carefree mood changed instantly. "Don't you be sayin' anything against yer dad. He's got his faults, like all of us do, but he was a good boy. He just never got much help when he was growin' up. Tommy, open the glove compartment an' give me that bottle."

I pushed a button, and the small, blue door fell open. The compartment was empty except for a rusted opener and a flat brown bottle. I gave the bottle to Grandpa.

"Is that medicine?" Fred asked.

"Best medicine there is. Cures everything a man's got if he uses enough of it." He uncorked the container, and the car slowly filled with a whiskey stench. He took several gulps, then shoved the bottle into his shirt pocket. "We got several miles to Hadleyville, men. Whatsay we shoot off a few explodin' crackers on the way?"

"While we're in the car?"

"Unless you wanna run alongside."

I wasn't sure what my grandfather had in mind, but having watched him hold a live firecracker in his hand, I knew he wasn't bluffing. As I reached into the bag, he pulled the cigarette lighter from the dashboard. The inside end glowed dull red. "I'll light it an' you toss it out the window," he said.

I took a good grip on the firecracker. As soon as the first spark leaped into the air, I sailed it past Fred's nose out the passenger window. It might have went off, or maybe it was a dud, we couldn't tell. Road noise from flying gravel covered all sounds past the rear of the car.

"Wait a little longer to throw it," Grandpa advised.

We made a second attempt. He slowed the car while the lighting took place. I counted to three this time before letting go, and it paid off; the firecracker exploded about a foot past the window.

"Ye gods," Fred yelled.

"Now we got it right," Grandpa said, grinning at me.

I shot off several more, with varying results, until Fred said he wanted to try it once. I laughed in his face, but Grandpa said he deserved an opportunity the same as me. If the old man had ever seen my uncoordinated brother in action, he might have decided otherwise.

With great reluctance I surrendered the middle position to Fred, taking over his window seat. I chose to sit with my back against the dashboard, allowing him a broader aim at the opening he needed to hit.

"Remember to count to three," I told him.

He nodded, and Grandpa lit the fuse.

"Onetwothree," screamed Fred, giving the firecracker a wild toss.

His misguided missile hit the doorpost and ricocheted into the backseat. The shocked expression on his face was the funniest I had seen since the time he dropped his toothbrush into the toilet.

"Where'd that one get to?" Grandpa asked, having to watch the road as a car passed us.

Before I could answer, the backseat blew up. My eardrums turned inside out as a cloud of dust and smoke rose from the rear of the car like a miniature Hiroshima. An empty beer can flew through the air and rattled against the back window. Fred was bawling before the echo died.

"I didn't mean to do it, Grandpa," he wailed.

Grandpa pulled the bottle from his pocket and drained half of what was left. Then he laughed. "What ya cryin' about, Boogernose? That was a great idea you had, throwin' a cracker into the backseat."

"It was?"

"You bet it was. That way we hear everything an' don't miss nothin'. Gimme another one of them things, Tommy."

He proceeded to light the firecracker, casually tossing it over his shoulder. Nagasaki fell.

By the time we reached Hadleyville, the bag was empty and the backseat was beyond description or repair. I mentioned the damage to Grandpa as we pulled into a parking area outside the carnival grounds. He shrugged, saying nobody ever sat back there anyway; we had enjoyed the destruction, so who cared? His care-free attitude might have been the whiskey beginning to work, but he was right about how much fun it had been throwing the firecrackers. I couldn't wait to tell Hippo about it, although he might not believe me. I wouldn't blame him, really.

Despite it being 10 o'clock on a Sunday morning, the carnival ground was packed. People bumped and pushed in all directions as we entered the main gate. Grandpa took hold of Fred's wrist; I kept one hand over the pocket containing our money. The air was full of calliope music and the pulsating roar of motors that powered the rides. But none of the sounds were too clear, as my ears still suffered the effects of the firecrackers. My nose was functioning properly, though, and it told me that cotton candy and taffy apples were being produced somewhere close by. It also mentioned that some of the jostling crowd had been too long without a bath.

"Can we ride the ferris wheel, Grandpa?" begged Fred.

"All day long if ya' want to."

We definitely wanted to. So we attached ourselves to a short line of people waiting to buy tickets on the Starlight Express, which was what the ride was actually called, according to a sign above the boarding ramp.

"Looks like it's twenty-five cents apiece," said Grandpa, digging into his pocket.

"I got money," I told him.

"Save it for flowers at my funeral."

"Yeah, but I want to pay for something."

"You can get the next one."

The Starlight Express slowed and came to a lurching, squeaking halt. One by one the seats were rotated and emptied, then immediately refilled with new passengers. The three of us crammed into a green seat with flaking paint. After the attendant locked the steel safety bar into place, we began a slow, jerking ascent. Beneath us, the rest of the line was absorbed into the wheel. Soon we could see much of the town of Hadleyville and the surrounding countryside.

We came to another stop just a few feet from the sky. Grandpa looked a little pale. "Wish they'd get this danged thing rollin'," he said.

"You okay?" I asked him.

"I'm fine. Just don't like heights too much. It ain't so bad if we're movin', but this hangin' around is no good. Junior's the same way when he gets off the ground."

There was that "Junior" business again.

"How come everybody down here calls Dad 'Junior'?"

"We've called him that since he was a little kid."

"But why?"

"It's his name, ya long-legged knucklehead. I'm Johnathon Kane Senior, an' he's Johnathon Kane Junior. If your name was Johnathon, you'd be Johnathon Kane the Third. Kinda scary, ain't it."

I felt like a fool. Thirteen years of living in the same house with my father, yet I didn't even know his full name. That pretty much summed up our whole relationship. I was glad the wheel had started moving again; it took my mind elsewhere.

For the next few minutes the breeze caressed my face, and a giddy sensation danced across my navel each time the Starlight Express began another revolution. Fred screamed incessantly. Grandpa was silent, but his fingerprints were carved into the safety bar. By the time we finished, he looked like he had spent six months in a jar of formaldehyde.

"I gotta sit a while," he moaned as we clattered down the exit ramp.

"We just got done sittin'," Fred said.

"Sittin' an' spinnin' is two different animals, Boogernose."

We escorted him to an overturned barrel behind the Tilt-a-Whirl. He drained the last of the whiskey, tossing the empty bottle to the ground.

"Feel better?" I asked.

"Some, but I need shade. Shoulda wore my hat, I guess."

His color had returned, but he was sweating profusely. Standing over him, I could see right through his thin, gray hair down to the scalp. His head looked very small.

"You want us to help you walk someplace?"

"Nah . . . I'll just rest here a while, then go to one of them tent shows an' see what they got. You two guys go ahead an' ride some of them crazy machines over there. I'll get ya some dough."

"It's my turn to pay," I reminded him.

"I got plenty," he said.

"Me too. We can take care of ourselves, don't worry. See you later, Grandpa."

"Meet me back here in an hour," he said, giving us a half-hearted wave.

I worried about him, but only until we came to the bumper cars. By the time my Jaguar rammed Fred's Corvette, I had forgotten Johnathon Kane Senior. After the cars, we rode something called the Slippery Snake. Next we slurped down blue snowcones. It was then that Fred informed me he wanted to carry his own money. I explained to him he only had five dollars, minus a quarter for the bumper cars, a quarter for the Snake, and a dime for the blue ice. It was only logical that I hold on to the rest so it wouldn't become lost.

"I want to carry it myself," he insisted.

"Listen, pellet brain, there's people at these carnivals just waiting for punks like you to come along. They'll get you hooked on one of their crooked games, and before you know it the money's gone. That's why it's better for somebody smart like me to hold it. Okay?"

"Gimme it, Tommy."

He stood in front of me, hands on hips, with blue tongue and lips, his pants half unzipped. Norman Rockwell might have appreciated such a defiant pose, but I was anxious to rid myself of his juvenile presence.

"Take your stinking money," I said, shoving four dollars and some change into his grubby palm. "But when it's gone, don't come crying to me. I hope somebody in one of them booths sucks you dry."

I might as well have talked to the clouds, because Fred squeezed the cash and disappeared into the crowd without bothering to answer. It felt good to be free of him. My spirit soared as I considered the possibilities of having almost thirty dollars in my pocket and nobody around to tell me how to spend it. I was ready for anything!

After a trip through the Spookhouse and a long look at a ninety-pound rat from the jungles of Peru, I decided to waste a quarter at the rifle shoot. A big guy, with a flat face and shoulders wide as a refrigerator took my money and handed me a rifle with a plastic stock.

"Knock down four in a row an' take anything I got," he said.

Among the prizes was a glass unicorn. Mom had mentioned how much she admired the glass animals in the parlor, so I decided it would be fun to help her start a collection of her own. I closed one eye and sighted down the rifle's barrel. A small figure arose in the back of the shooting gallery.

"Meet Pretty Boy Floyd," the guy said as if introducing a close friend.

I touched the trigger and sent Floyd to the Promised Land, or wherever metallic mobsters go. Baby Face Nelson popped up to take his place and met a similar fate. I took a breath and waited for the next fool to step forward; it was John Dillinger. I had read about him once in a magazine. He had been Public Enemy Number One, and yet a lot of people considered him a hero. Hero or villain, he meant nothing to me. I blew him away.

"One more an' you got it," the big guy assured me, picking his teeth with a piece of wire.

"Who is it this time?"

"Bonnie an' Clyde."

"Two of 'em?"

"You hit the target, it'll fall. This ain't no gyp-joint, kid."

Taking careful aim, I fired the last shot. Bonnie and Clyde took the hit, quivered, and lived to fight another day.

"Tough luck there, kid. Wanna try again?"

I knew the fourth shot had been as accurate as the first three. Any further attempts at winning would be money wasted, but I felt reckless.

"One more time," I said.

He gave me a different gun, and I slid another quarter across the counter. The same three criminals arose from the dead, only to be shot down again. Then once more it was me against Bonnie and Clyde for the right to possess a glass unicorn. It seemed a logical assumption that the fourth target was balanced differently from the others, allowing it to absorb the impact of a shot and remain standing. Perhaps the key was to aim somewhere other than dead center. I lowered my sight to the base of the figure and shot the last round. It had the same effect as a marshmallow thrown against the Rock of Gibraltar.

"Ain't that somethin'," said the guy as if he honestly could not understand why my last shot kept failing. "Maybe you'll get it next time."

"Heck with it," I said.

He tried talking me into one more attempt, but my mind was made up. Whatever it took to beat the system was beyond me, and I knew it. Mom would just have to start her collection with something other than a glass unicorn. But as I turned to walk away, he called me back.

"You're a good sport, slim, so I'm givin' you a free ticket to the Wheel of Winners game. It's right down there on the end, same side as me."

"Hey, thanks!"

He shrugged as if it was nothing, and I knew he was probably right. When a guy gets something free, he can usually figure it's worthless, or else it has a mile-long string attached someplace. Still, it wouldn't hurt to check the situation over; what could that cost me?

The Wheel of Winners was right next to Hector the Runaway Mouse, a nimble, gray rodent scampering through a maze with eight separate exits. Each exit was a different color, and bets were placed on which one Hector would choose. The customers playing the game at that moment were all females. Every time the mouse made an appearance they screamed, as if terrified to be so close to such a creature. I wished I could have smuggled the ninety-pound rat from Peru into Hector's cage and watched the excitement when they saw his ugly face pop out of the hole!

"Can I help you, honey?" someone asked.

I turned away from the crowd at Hector's to face a stunning woman with blonde hair and a dark tan. She leaned across the counter of the Wheel of Winners booth, wearing a yellow halter top with matching shorts. Her teeth were square and white, like the sides of sugar cubes, as she smiled.

"I got a free ticket," I mumbled, my mouth suddenly dry.

"Well, that's great. Who knows, this may be your lucky day, mister."

Mister? She obviously thought I was a man, and that was exciting, especially coming from a woman bearing strong resemblance to Marilyn Monroe!

"What I gotta do?" I asked her.

"Just let me have the ticket and you can give the wheel a spin."

That I did, and the wheel nearly twisted off its axle. The numbers painted upon it became blurred, appearing to spin backward.

"Oooh, you're strong," cooed the blonde.

"Yeah, sorta."

We waited in silence until the numbers became clear again. When the wheel finally stopped, the pointer was at 50.

"I knew it," the blonde said, "you're Mr. Lucky. You're halfway to the big prize without even buying a ticket!"

"What is the big prize?"

She pointed to a silver transistor radio in the back of the booth. It looked expensive. Wouldn't Fred die if I came back with that fancy machine. Such a thought was worth the price of a ticket.

"How much to play?"

"Quarter."

I gave her the money and spun the wheel again. This time it came to rest on a golden, wedge-shaped space marked BONUS. The blonde threw up her hands. "I don't believe this."

"What happened?"

She reached under the counter and pulled out a black metal box. "That bonus is worth big money," she said, counting five twenties and laying them in front of me.

"I get all that?"

"Plus the radio, if you win . . . I mean *when* you win." She winked at me, and I got goosebumps handing her another quarter. "Oh darn," she said, "I forgot about the price increase."

"What price increase?"

"It's a house rule, honey. After a bonus the price is a dollar a spin."

"Oh."

A dollar per spin sounded pretty expensive, but I was already halfway to the big prize after spending only twenty-five cents. A guy could buy a lot of spins and still have most of that hundred in his pocket when the dust cleared. What was a few bucks to someone only fifty points away from a fortune?

"Hit another good one, lover," the blonde said, shoving my dollar into the money belt around her waist.

Lover? I gave the wheel a twist that nearly made the Richter scale. It stopped on 20.

"That's seventy," said the blonde, palm out. The next spin added nine points to the total. Another dollar got me to eighty-six. By then I had to break a five, but felt no pain. Fourteen more points and it was all mine: the money, the radio, and maybe even the blonde if I was any judge of women. She was definitely hooked on me.

"Be there, baby," I yelled as the wheel began another turn. It was appropriate to say such a thing; I had seen Clark Gable do it in a movie when he rolled dice. But even Clark never owned such luck as I was experiencing. The wheel once again came to rest upon BONUS.

"Oh my gosh," moaned the blonde. "I never saw anybody hit that thing twice!"

The metal box made another appearance. Five more twenties lined the counter.

"I get that too?"

"You sure do, handsome. You'll have enough to take me out for dinner and a night on the town."

Dinner? Me and the blonde? The dollar almost vibrated out of my hand. I was nearly delirious with joy, but she seemed hesitant.

"There is one bad thing about getting another bonus, baby-doll."

"What's that?"

"Well, from now on it costs five dollars to spin the wheel."

"Five dollars! What kind of ripoff operation are you running here, woman?"

The blonde acted as if she was close to tears.

"It's not my fault. I just do what I'm told. If it was up to me, I'd give you the prize right now because you're going to win it anyway."

I was ashamed. The young lady had been so friendly, had treated me so well, and now I had insulted her integrity. Guys like me belonged in a shooting gallery between Baby Face Nelson and Dillinger.

"I'm sorry. Just seeing all that money got me a little excited. Here's the five."

She took the money and gave me the most fabulous smile ever formed on the face of a human being. It diminished only slightly when the wheel stopped on 6.

"That's ninety-two, honey! Ooh, you're so close I can hardly stand it. Once more and it's over."

I dug into my billfold and found one more five. The green was beginning to thin out, and I noticed the blonde eyeing my reserves. I turned away to perform a quick audit. Only seventeen dollars remained, but that was more than enough to win the prize.

"Kiss for luck?" asked the blonde.

Kiss? Even in my comatose condition I must have nodded in the affirmative, because she leaned across the counter and nuzzled my cheek. For a while I didn't know what century it was. I had no memory of spinning the wheel, but that was insignificant because it was rotating and beginning to slow down. The blonde gave a loud scream.

"Did I get it?" I asked, still somewhat foggy.

"Take a look, moneybags."

I hadn't won the prize, but the next best thing had happened. By some miracle the wheel once again rested on BONUS! The metal box only had three twenties left, so the blonde dug out four tens. I was considering changing my last name to Rockefeller when a disturbing thought crept into my mind.

"What's it cost to play after the third bonus?" I asked.

The blonde pursed her lips in dismay. "I sure hate to say so, baby, but it's twenty dollars."

My stomach churned as if it intended to erupt in the near future.

"I don't have twenty dollars!"

"Oh, honey, don't say that."

"It's the truth. I only got seventeen bucks and some change."

I proved it by emptying out my billfold and pockets. She ran a pink-tipped finger across my meager mound of money. A strange smile formed on her lips.

"We've got a problem here, sweety. The rules won't let me keep the game going if you can't come up with the full price."

"Yeah, but I'm only a couple bucks short. I'll go ahead and win it with this spin, and then you'll get your money."

She looked doubtful.

"It could cost me my job if they catch me, lover. I mean, a girl can't throw her future away on the first good-looking guy who comes along. If you had something like a watch to go along with the money, maybe we could work out a deal."

"I don't have a watch."

"What about that?" She pointed to Jimmy's ring.

"No way! I got that from a friend, and I'm keeping it."

"Some girl, I bet," she pouted.

"It was a guy."

Her eyebrows raised. "You're not one of those fruity-fruitcake types, are you?"

"He was just a good friend, that's all."

"Sure he was . . . That's why you'll never part with it. Sounds fishy to me."

The excitement of the prize money, the closeness of the blonde, and the humid weather had forced my sweat glands to over-achieve. My strength turned to saltwater. I felt like I had just carried Hippo Reeves on my back across Death Valley. The whole thing had gone on too long, and I wanted it to be ended. The ring came off my slippery finger. I hoped Jimmy, wherever he was, would understand.

"Take it," I told the blonde.

She looked around, making sure nobody was watching.

"Okay, honey, let's get it this time."

It would take 8 or better to win. I gave the wheel a final spin, making a silent plea for victory to whatever forces might be listening at that moment.

The wheel turned forever. Spiders wove intricate webs in the far corners of the booth while we waited. Civilizations rose and fell, rivers cut new channels through the earth, and distant stars went nova as the numbers chased each other. Then, almost without our knowing, it stopped. The pointer, a paper-thin strip of tarnished copper, was hung up on the dividing marker between five and ten. It vibrated like a plucked guitar string. The tension level went beyond my capacity to endure.

"Hit 10," I screamed.

Maybe it was air currents from my big mouth, or maybe just bad luck, but the pointer made a soft twang and came to rest on the orange-colored number 5.

"Oh no!" cried the blonde. "That's just terrible, honey!"

"I don't have any more money," I said, as if she didn't know.

"You just had some tough luck, baby. You'll do better next time."

I watched her remove the stacks of green from the counter. She didn't seem to realize the enormity of what had happened. I was broke! Sucked dry by a stupid game!

"Next time! Forget about next time . . . I gotta keep going right now."

The blonde's face wasn't as friendly as before.

"No money, no play," she said.

"I'll get the money. My grandpa is around here somewhere . . . I can get it from him. Just hold my place until I get back."

"I can't do that. The rules say if a person leaves, the game is over."

"Yeah, but couldn't you just—"

"Look, you little toad, it's over. You lost, so forget about it."

Little toad? The truth hit me between the eyes like a bullet from the rifle shoot. This had all been a put-on. I was just another sucker to this woman. She had fluttered her eyelids, laid some cash in front of me, and I handed over my life's savings to her like a hick from McKinley, Iowa. Now that I was broke, she was finished with me, and I was expected to just move peacefully along without making a scene. Forget that!

"You're a stinking cheat!" I screamed at her. "Give me my money back or I'll tear this place apart!"

I hoped such an outburst might startle or embarrass her into returning my losses, but she had played the game before. A quick grab under the counter produced a short section of chain.

"Make one dumb move and I'll brain you, brainless."

I had no doubt she would. We glared across the counter at each other as a door opened in the rear of the booth. The big guy from the rifle shoot hulked inside.

"What's the deal?" he rumbled.

The blonde ran to him, hanging herself upon his granite shoulders. "This creep is threatening to beat me up."

"Oh yeah?"

He shoved her aside, charging the counter like a wounded rhino. I wasn't sure if he intended going over, around, or through the obstacle in his path, and I didn't wait to find out. Forsaking honor for existence, I turned and ran. After changing directions twenty times and bouncing off a dozen people, I realized the enemy had abandoned the chase. It was safe to flop down on a pile of straw bales behind the pony rides.

I rested for nearly fifteen minutes, giving my befuddled brain a chance to gather itself. I reconstructed the events at the Wheel of Winners and considered what, if anything, could be done. A measure of mental revenge was attained by imagining myself burning the booth and karate-chopping the bruiser into submission. I was about to slap the blonde when Fred's voice brought me back to reality.

"Hey, Tommy, look what I won."

He was carrying a glass unicorn.

"Where'd you get that?"

"At the shooting place. I killed a bunch of people—I forget who they was—an' I got this horse. Mom will like it, huh!"

That was the final humiliation. While I handed my money over to the blonde barracuda, my dumb brother had won the unicorn for Mom. His success doubled my failure, and it had been large enough already. I wanted to go home.

"You seen Grandpa?" I asked.

"Uh uh."

The overturned barrel where we left him was diagonally across from us, but he wasn't there. The hour had long since expired.

"Let's move around and see if we can find him," I said.

We walked until our feet felt like link sausages sliding across a hot skillet. We searched everywhere on the carnival grounds except the women's restroom. We checked back at the car and roamed the entire parking lot. He had vanished. Fred said he was worried about Grandpa. So was I.

The distant courthouse clock sounded noon, then half past. Our skin began to redden. We retired to the car to escape the sun's cruel glare. The slight breeze kept the inside temperature below the danger level. Barely.

"I'm hungry," Fred whined for the tenth time.

"Grandpa will be back soon."

"You said that an hour ago."

I had no desire to argue. My throat felt like a piece of sandpaper, and the words kept getting roughed up as they came out. Concern for Grandpa was being replaced by anger. Where had he gone? Didn't he realize we were alone in a strange town? Didn't he care what happened to us?

"Hey!" Fred yelled.

"Now what?"

"Where's all your money? You had a whole bunch when we came, an' I'll bet you still got it. You're just mad because I won something for Mom, so now you won't buy me nothing to eat. You're a stingy pig, Tommy."

"I lost all the money."

"Huh?"

"You deaf? I said I lost it."

"How?"

"At the Wheel of Winners. They got Jimmy's ring too."

Fred's gaze dropped to my left hand. "Did you cry?"

"Crying don't get the money back," I said, trying to sound tough, but remembering how close I had actually been to tears.

Shortly past 1, our black Buick pulled up behind Grandpa's Chevy. The Chief stepped out of the passenger door, meeting us between the two cars.

"Where is your grandfather?" he asked coldly.

"We haven't seen him for a couple hours," I said.

"Was he drinking?"

"Yes, sir."

"We're starving to death, Chief," Fred said. "I spent all my money, an' Tommy lost his at a game, so we couldn't get nothing to eat."

Dad was out of the Buick by then. "You lost all your vacation money?"

"And Jimmy's ring too," said the ever-helpful Fred.

"Where did this happen?" the Chief asked me.

"At a booth called the Wheel of Winners."

"Show me."

As we left, the Chief ordered Dad to buy some sandwiches for us to eat on the trip home. Dad took Fred and did as he was told. The Chief and I then returned to the sight of my monetary massacre. The blonde and her boyfriend were counting the contents of the metal box.

"Who's in charge here?" demanded the Chief.

"I call the shots," said the big guy. "So what?"

"I think you were pretty rough on this boy."

The two crooks looked at me; their faces were a mixture of amusement and contempt.

"We didn't send out no engraved invitations," the guy said. "The kid came of his own free will an' spent the money because he wanted to. Nobody twisted his arm."

The Chief stared the guy straight in the eye, his voice low yet authoritative.

"You didn't twist any arms, but I have a feeling that you and her like to twist that wheel a little bit when the time is right."

The big guy's face got red.

"Look here, Pop, I don't—"

The Chief slammed his cane across the counter. The blonde jumped a foot.

"My name is Kane, not Pop, and I say you cheated this boy out of something which belongs to him. And I also say this is Pettis County, Missouri, and the Sheriff is like a son to me. If I put a bug in his ear, you and your friend are out of business."

The big guy considered for a moment, then shrugged. "We leave in a few hours for the next county anyhow, so I don't figure it makes much difference who you know."

"Which county is that?"

"Benton."

The Chief gave him an icy smile.

"Bill Hanks is the Sheriff over in Benton County. Him and I spend a week every fall in the Ozarks, fishing. I'll see if maybe he can't find a way to stick a nail in your wheel. Sort of smooth out those fancy hops it makes."

The big guy stared at his feet. I knew he was whipped.

"I don't want no trouble over a few bucks some punk lost," he said. "How much you drop, kid?"

"About thirty-five."

"About thirty, you little skunk," said the blonde.

Little skunk? It didn't sound like she loved me anymore. Women could be so fickle.

"You people keep the money," said the Chief, to my astonishment.

The big guy was as surprised as I. "I don't get you."

"The boy was stupid enough to throw away his money at a place like this, so he will pay for that mistake. But he also lost a ring, and that is what I want returned."

"Ring?"

"This dumb thing," said the blonde, pulling it from the back pocket of her yellow shorts and flipping it onto the counter. "Looks like it came out of a Cracker Jack box. Big deal."

"Pick it up," the Chief ordered me.

After I grabbed the ring, his cane returned to the ground.

"In the future," he said, "I hope you people find a better line of work than taking money from fools."

The big guy looked at me and laughed.

"Suckers are big business, an' somebody's gotta milk 'em. Might as well be us."

The Chief turned his back on the three of us and walked away. As I took a final look at the blonde, she made a gesture confirming that she was no lady. I was glad to be seeing the last of her. Not only had she fleeced me, she also made me a fool in the Chief's estimation. I hurried to catch up with him, knowing the shame of this day would last a long time.

Dad and Fred were waiting in the Buick. Fred was eating a hamburger and had ketchup smeared on his chin.

"We got one for you, Tommy," he said, hanging out the window.

The Chief snapped his fingers to get Dad's attention. "Pick us up at Pat's Place."

"Yes, sir," Dad said. Evidently he was in almost as much trouble as me.

Before I could reach for my hamburger, the Chief poked me in the rear with the tip of his cane, moving me toward the street. It made me mad to be prodded like some cow, but I was in no position to do anything other than respond meekly to his leading. When we reached the curb, I saw a tavern on the other side of the road. A sign along the top of the building read, Pat's Place. I had a fair idea who we expected to find inside that joint, and it wasn't Jackie Kennedy!

Compared to the July sunlight, it was midnight inside Pat's Place. My eyes took a while to adjust. The Chief walked to the bar where a man pouring drinks pointed to a booth in the back of the room. It was there we found Grandpa, staring down at an empty shot glass.

"Hit me again," he slurred without looking up.

"If hitting you again would help, I'd beat you senseless," said the Chief.

Grandpa's head rolled rather than turned in our direction. He appeared confused, like he was trying to remember something.

"I'm amazed to see ya, Poppa," he said. His tongue sounded like it had become too big for his mouth.

The Chief ignored him and spoke to me.

"I wanted you to see him for what he really is—a worthless, spineless drunkard. You kids don't mean a thing to him compared to liquor. He left you and Fredric alone to come here and drink booze. One Sunday a year they allow this tavern to stay open to catch the carnival trade, and he's right here to take full advantage. The next time he comes to tempt you away from your responsibilities, I want you to consider what you see here. He has chosen the life of a bum, and this is what it looks like. Today all you lost was a little money, but if a boy continues down the wrong path, this is his final destination. Remember that, Thomas Jamison."

Grandpa watched me through red, watery eyes.

"We had us some fun, ol' Tommy toughstuff," he mumbled, reaching a hand toward me.

The Chief used his cane to push Grandpa's arm back down to the table. "Whatever you touch dies, boy, so keep your hand on a bottle where it belongs."

Grandpa put his head down and began to cry. "I wish it could have been me," he sobbed.

"So do I. I've wished it every day for fifty-four years."

I wasn't sure what they were talking about, but there was no time to find out. The Chief gave me another jab with his cane, herding me back outside into the fierce sunlight where Dad and Fred sweated inside the Buick.

"Are we just going to leave him like that?" I asked.

"You can pull a pig from the mud, Thomas Jamison, and it runs right back as soon as you leave. So why bother? Get in the car."

Except for Fred's bragging about winning the glass unicorn, the trip back to Climer was made in silence. The atmosphere was oppressive. The Chief's anger surrounded us like a set of black curtains. The hamburger stuck in my throat until we reached the hotel.

A bath and some skin lotion cooled my outer body, but inside I remained hot with shame. Thanks to Fred, my unfortunate encounter at the Wheel of Winners became common knowledge. The day's events were rehashed several times as each new listener had to be informed of Tommy's folly. The Chief was generously praised for rescuing Fred and me and the ring; Grandpa was spoken of in hushed tones accompanied by solemn head shaking. Fred was given credit for being a "brave little man." The glass unicorn sat in a place of honor on a dining room shelf. I had been allowed to live, but the vote was very close.

After the evening meal the rest of the family twirled sparklers on the front porch, enjoying the splendor of an orange and lavender sunset. I stayed in bedroom number 6 watching the empty streets of Climer dissolve into shapeless stretches of twilight.

Occasionally the muffled sound of laughter floated upward through the branches of an ancient oak outside the window. I longed to share in the happiness below, but I was mad at everyone in the universe. Nobody could be trusted. The blonde had played me for a sucker, Grandpa deserted me, and the Chief had said I was a fool and allowed those cheaters to keep my money. My parents had offered no sympathy whatsoever. Even the aunts had tsk-tsked when they found out what I had done. I felt isolated, an outcast from the human race. I needed someone to hear my troubles, someone to tell me things were going to be all right. But there didn't seem to be anyone who cared about me, not anywhere in the world.

MISSOURI

I assumed the Chief would never speak to me again after the carnival fiasco, but that was not true. The next morning, just past 8, Julia and Inez were setting out dishes for the next meal while I finished my bowl of Sugar Frosted Flakes.

"Are you sure that's all you're going to have?" worried Julia. "I can whip up an egg in a jiffy."

"No thank you, Julia."

She shook her head and left the room talking to herself about not trusting those boxes of sweet-flavored things kids were eating nowadays. Inez stood at the far end of the table removing a blue sugar bowl and matching salt and pepper shakers from a silver tray. The hotel was unusually quiet.

"Where's everybody at?" I asked her.

"Well, your parents took Freddy into Sedalia to do a little shopping."

"Oh."

For a moment I wondered why I had not been asked to go along; then yesterday came to mind. No doubt I was grounded, and who could guess what else. Inez must have read my mind.

"Poppa wanted you to stay here today. You're supposed to meet him at the cemetery when you finish eating."

"Cemetery?"

"Yes . . . The family plots are at the very backside of our property, behind the row of cedar trees."

I was vaguely familiar with the row of cedar trees, but not with the cemetery.

"What does the Chief want me for?"

Inez looked puzzled. "I never thought to ask."

That didn't surprise me. People never seemed to question anything the Chief did or said. I hadn't decided whether or not to hate him, but I definitely knew better than to antagonize him two days in a row. The sooner I went to him, the quicker I might crawl out of his doghouse.

When Inez wasn't looking, I tipped my bowl and gulped the remainder of the mushy flakes. My forearm served as a napkin.

"I'm going now, Aunt Inez."

"All right, dear, but be careful not to shake up your breakfast."

She and Julia were forever warning me to move slowly after meals so as not to disturb the digestive system. Such a thing was bad for the complexion, according to some Dr. Foley. I found out later that Dr. Foley died just before Pearl Harbor, but his theories lived on.

On this hazy morning I was content to obey the auntly admonition and walk slowly toward the row of cedars. The air was warm and close as I crossed the expanse of green in front of the trees. Flowers were in full-bloom all around me, and bees floated lazily from one bunch to another in search of sweetness. A bobwhite told me his name from a nearby lilac bush.

The Chief was nowhere to be seen. What did he want with me, and why had he chosen to meet me in a cemetery? Surely he didn't have the right to kill me for past mistakes and deposit my remains in a prepared grave. That seemed a little out of line, even in Climer, Missouri!

It was difficult to see beyond the cedars because the shadows they created were such a contrast to the white sunlight. Waist-high clumps of foliage grew between the trees—mostly raspberry bushes and some rhubarb. I found an opening in the flora that led to an area filled with giant sunflowers. They towered over me by more than a foot. Their brown centers were as big as my head, and the yellow petals grew finger-sized.

"I'm glad you could make it, Thomas Jamison."

The Chief had materialized from someplace and now stood an

arm's length away. On his head was a dressy straw hat appearing to be left over from some vaudeville act.

"Inez said you wanted me."

"Yes. I've got something for you to see."

He stepped into the wall of sunflowers. I followed and saw a narrow pathway stretching ahead of us. Rough, green leaves, the size of footballs, clung to my clothing as we walked. Suddenly the patch of sunflowers opened to reveal several tombstones resting in a space about thirty feet square.

"This is where we come when our work is finished," said the Chief.

His way of describing death sounded funny to me, but I only nodded and tried to look serious. I was curious to know who was buried in this place, so I examined the closest stone. It was gray and rectangular, with the name KANE chiseled at the top in large letters. Underneath the family title two smaller names were visible. The first, belonging to the Chief, was followed by the date 1874. The other name was Eleanor Kane; the dates were 1876-1948. I thought of her portrait in the parlor and wished someone would invite me inside for a closer look at my great-grandmother.

"Thirteen years," said the Chief.

"Huh?"

"I said it's been thirteen years since she passed away—thirteen this month. Doesn't seem that long, but then again there are times it feels like she's been gone forever. She was quite a lady."

He was leaning on his cane, his gnarled, blue-veined hands squeezing the neck. Flared ends of his white mustache quivered in the breeze as he stared at the tombstone.

"Do you believe in God, Thomas Jamison?"

The question surprised me. On a hot Summer morning, in a tiny cemetery surrounded by giant sunflowers, with memories of his wife whispering to him, the man asked me about God. At another time, with a little more warning, I might have given a more diplomatic answer, one which didn't sound so final.

"No."

His eyes remained upon the headstone; his expression was unchanged.

"That doesn't surprise me. You come from a recent line of men who have chosen to disregard their Creator. You even bear the name of one whose doubt was recorded by the Scriptures."

"I do?" I had no idea what he was talking about.

"Do you think me a fool, young man?"

"No, sir."

"Well, I believe in God."

His words hung in the air like Grandpa's whiskey breath. I didn't know what he expected me to say. I couldn't think. My brain was an empty room with the door bolted shut.

"God is just something for old people when they're afraid to die," I said.

Such a statement drew his gaze toward me, and I was shocked at my own words. They were merely a repetition of what Dad once told me during a drunken lecture. I hadn't meant them to be insulting, but no doubt the Chief would see them as such.

"Your father taught you that, I assume?"

It would have been easy to drag Dad into the mud with me. He already seemed scared to death of offending the old man, and certainly didn't need my help to reserve a seat in the doghouse.

"I . . . He didn't actually say . . ."

"You just said I'm not a fool, Thomas Jamison, so don't expect me to think like one. Those words came from your father, who heard them from your grandfather, who definitely never heard them from me. They are lies, and my only concern is that you have a chance to hear the truth. Let's sit over here while we talk."

He pointed to a large section of tree trunk lying on the ground to our left. A rough seat had been hacked out of the top which easily held us both. The air was now dead, befitting our surroundings. The sweet smells of hot grass and sunflower leaves were almost suffocating.

"I'm eighty-six years old now," he said, "but my belief in God began at a young age, despite whatever theories your father or grandfather may have. God is real, and it doesn't matter how old people are. They need Him."

"If there's a God, then why would He let a kid be killed for no reason?"

I couldn't believe how these things kept rolling out of my mouth. All I really wanted to do was get back on the Chief's good side, but I was trying to extinguish a fire with gasoline.

"Look over here," he said, struggling to his feet and walking to another of the tombstones. This one was older and smaller. The stone was dirty-white, and the lettering was wearing away. KANE was barely visible above the inscription BELOVED SON. I knelt down to get a better look. As best I could tell, it read PAUL 1897-1907. "He was my second son, Paul Jamison Kane."

I felt strange hearing that this long-dead boy had the same middle name as me. Perhaps that was part of the reason the Chief insisted on hooking Jamison to Thomas every time he spoke my name.

"What happened to him?" I asked.

"Like you just said, he was killed for no reason. Just a careless accident that took my precious boy from me."

There were tears in his blue eyes. I wanted to turn away, but could not. What kind of pain must that tough old man have felt to cry about something happening over fifty years ago? Emotional encounters had almost become commonplace the past two weeks, but seeing the Chief like this was hard to handle.

"I'm sorry," I said. If he heard, he gave no indication.

"You lost a friend recently, didn't you, Thomas Jamison?"

"Yes, sir . . . Jimmy Swailes."

"And because of that you are mad at God, is that correct?"

"Well, it just doesn't seem fair."

"No, I suppose it doesn't. When I carried Paul into the hotel the day he was killed, I didn't think it was fair that other boys lived while he lay dead. I heard Eleanor's screams and asked God how He could have permitted such a thing to happen. But never did I turn against the Almighty. He gave me a son, and He had the right to take him back. Do you understand?"

"I'm not sure."

The Chief took the end of his cane and knocked a fat grasshopper off the top of his son's tombstone.

"God is not accountable to human beings for what He does. The Good Book says His thoughts and reasons are far beyond anything we can understand. Just take that grasshopper there . . . I could have picked him up and told him I would rather he didn't sit on that marker and spit juice all over it, but he wouldn't understand. I could tell him for a hundred years and he wouldn't understand, so I just went ahead and moved him. Sometimes God does the same thing with us.

"Yeah, but we're a lot smarter than bugs."

"True . . . But compared to Him, we know very little."

"If God is so smart, then why don't He make everything good instead of letting it be rotten all the time?"

"He will, boy, when the time is right. People are impatient. If they don't get things right away, they forget about God. But the wonderful thing is that He doesn't forget about us. Even after we are dead and buried, He remembers."

I must have looked skeptical about that last statement because he stepped closer, poking a finger against my chest.

"There are nights, young man, when I dream of my Eleanor, and I'll remember something that time has removed from my mind over the years. Many times I've dreamed how her hair smelled one afternoon when we got caught in the rain during haying season. She was handling the horses while I forked hay into the wagon. It was terrible hot, so when the sky got dark and drops started hitting us, we drove the wagon into the barn and then walked together in the rain. Her damp hair smelled a certain way that I could never begin to describe. In my dreams I can call back that wonderful smell for a few seconds, but then I lose it again. Sometimes I lose the gold specks in her green eyes, or the sound of her singing while she did chores around the house. I've almost lost the memory of just holding her hand as we walked the prairie at sundown. She loved to pick the little blue periwinkle flowers. They were her favorite, and you'll notice I've planted them around her marker.

"One of these days I'll be gone, and there won't be a person left in the world who remembers Eleanor Jamison Kane when she was twenty years old. Except God. And He has promised there will come a day when she will rise up and be given a brand-new body that can never grow old. I'm trusting Him to keep that promise. Now you'll have to excuse me, Thomas Jamison. I need to go lie down."

He turned away, leaving me astonished at what had been said about his wife getting a new body. That sounded like reincarnation or voodoo or some such business. Thoughts of Dracula and half-rotted ghouls passed through my mind, but I dismissed them as mere cemetery fantasies. The Chief had obviously drained himself talking about deceased loved ones. All that new body stuff was just wishful thinking.

At the edge of the sunflower path he stopped, slowly looking back at me. For the first time since I met him, he truly resembled a man in his eighties.

"I almost forgot why I brought you out here," he said. "I need someone to pull weeds around the graves and mow this patch of ground. If you are interested, there are tools in the shed behind the garage. I pay five dollars, and I expect a good job."

Then he was gone, leaving me alone among relatives I had never known. I took a look at each of the headstones. It was fun imagining what those people might have been like and what they had done with their lives. I thought of steely-eyed sheriffs and heroic soldiers, but doubtless my ancestors were people of the commonest professions. Climer didn't seem a likely place for men of renown to gather in death.

After the cemetery tour was completed, I retraced my steps to the hotel to get the necessary tools for carrying out grounds-keeping chores. The next three hours I clipped, uprooted, and mowed around the resting-places of my family, working like never before to make the area acceptable in the Chief's sight. My final task, as I prepared to leave the cemetery, was to remove another grasshopper from atop the marker of Paul Jamison Kane. Instead of simply knocking it off, I picked the creature up with my hand and pretended to be God. I ordered it to never again trespass upon sacred ground. The grasshopper responded by making a brown spot upon my palm. I hurled the blasphemer to the ground, squashing it with my shoe. Tom Kane would make one tough God, believe that!

• • • •

The air inside the hotel almost felt cool after my hours in the sun. A quick check of the refrigerator showed that Julia's famous pink lemonade had become extinct, but the dear old girl must have heard me praising the taste of Dr. Pepper because the door tray held at least a dozen bottles. I slurped on one of them while heading to the bathroom to prepare a tub of cool water. A shower would have been preferable, but the hotel had none to offer.

Halfway down the hall the smell of perfume told me Belle had already set up camp. I found her leaning close to the mirror, applying green eye shadow. The stuff made her lids look as if they had been transplanted from a lizard. She saw my reflection in the mirror; one corner of her mouth turned upward.

"If it isn't the high roller himself. Looks like you've been sweating."

"I've been working."

"Is that a fact? Can I assume you were doing the Chief's bidding?"

"Yeah . . . He had me fixing up the cemetery."

Belle laughed a cynical laugh. "If that old relic worried as much about the living as he does those stupid graves, we would all be a lot better off around here."

I didn't know what to say, so I finished my soda and watched her construct a new face. She plucked her eyebrows, rubbed an orange powder onto her cheeks, and added another layer of purple-red lipstick. I noticed that her lacy-cuffed robe was the same shade of yellow as what the blonde at the carnival had worn. It was likely they had more in common than just the color of their clothes.

"How old do you think I am?" she asked.

"I dunno."

"Guess."

Figuring her age was difficult. She didn't look as old as Mom, but I knew many tricks were used to make her appear younger. The past ten minutes confirmed that.

"Thirty-five," I said, just to shut her up.

She threw back her head and laughed. I saw the fillings in her teeth.

"You wouldn't be trying to flatter me, would you?"

"Not really."

Again she laughed. "Regardless of intent, you have done exactly that. The truth is, I'm within a few months of becoming an ancient fifty."

"Fifty!"

"Half a century. To some people around here that's not much more than a baby, but it's still a lot of pages to tear off the calendar. Too many to suit me, kiddo."

"Have you always lived here?"

"No. Like most of the inmates in this asylum, I am a transplant—one of the Chief's projects."

"Projects?"

"Of course. You see, we aren't worthy of the good life at the hotel in our flawed condition, so that old man tries to straighten us out with his religious folderol. It's all a waste of time because some of us are hopelessly wicked and not about to be changed. But the Chief still beats the drum. Ask your father or grandfather about it sometime."

"Is that why everybody's scared of the Chief?"

"Not everyone is scared, thank you."

"Are you?"

She began putting her powders and facial machinery into a tan leather case. "Let's just say I'm smart enough to know it takes money to get along in this world. For the time being, that old man's got the checkbook in his hand, so I play along. But I should ask you the same question. You probably got one of his fire and brimstone specials this morning—did it scare you?"

"I get nervous every time he shows up, especially after yesterday. I can't even figure out if he likes me or not."

"Don't hold your breath waiting for good news. I've been around him most of my life and still haven't gotten a friendly word. It's not his way to treat people like anything but cheap help."

"Yeah, but Julia and Inez like him."

Belle gave her face a final scrutiny in the mirror. "He is their father, you know. Besides, those two would have thought Hitler was just a nice German boy who worried too much about Jews. It's all yours, kiddo. I'm finished."

I watched as she glided away from me in a flowing robe and fluffy yellow slippers. A strange mixture of elegance and venom was Cousin Belle. She could probably provide me with answers to some of the questions concerning my relatives, but I didn't trust her.

Half an hour in the tub cooled me and put me to sleep. I awoke, with a startled splash, to the distant strains of a piano. After a quick lather and rinse, I put on the same dirty clothes and sneaked upstairs to find something clean to wear.

The bedroom was stuffy despite open windows. Curtains hung limp, and flies clung listlessly to the screens, as if trying to regain strength sapped by the merciless sun. I was reminded of similar conditions inside the Buick yesterday while we waited for Grandpa. Had he made it home all right? Was he sorry for deserting us? I tried convincing myself that I should still be mad at him, but I couldn't. There was something about that little man which made me like him despite his many weaknesses.

By the time I found clean clothes and got back downstairs, my body was sweating as much as before the bath. I soon discovered that the piano music was being produced by Belle. I watched through the parlor doors as she played, her back toward me, with great intensity. The music was unfamiliar, but it must have been composed by an angry man judging by the way she pounded the keys. Upon completion she turned as if expecting a visitor.

"Don't just stand there with your face hanging out," she said, like I really didn't need an invitation to enter the room.

The glass knob felt cold as I opened the door. For some reason the poem about the spider and the fly came to mind.

"Should I close this door again?"

"Please."

The parlor was even more impressive than I had realized. It smelled like manners and class, if that was possible. Each piece of furniture looked as if it had been purchased that very day. The hardwood floor was almost a mirror.

"This place is cool," I said.

"Then why are you perspiring?"

"I just meant that I really like it."

"I know perfectly well what you meant. I was being clever."

She laughed as if she had looked inside my head and become amused at the amount of unoccupied space found there. I didn't like it, and chose to ignore her. My attention was given to the imposing gilded portrait of Eleanor Kane.

"That is an excellent likeness of Grandmother," Belle said.

"She's so young."

"About twenty-five, I should think. The Chief had it done not too long after the hotel was built. He gave a traveling artist a free week of room and board in exchange for the portrait. I don't know what ever became of Mr. Henry Martz, but he certainly left his mark on our little corner of the planet."

The woman in the painting seemed alive, like I was looking at her through a window. Her green eyes stared deeply into mine. The tresses of honey-brown hair would surely move should a breeze blow through the room. It was possible to imagine the faint rustling of fabric as she took each breath. Eleanor Kane had been beautiful. I understood quite well why the Chief wanted captured in oil what his mind might someday be unable to hold.

"Was she nice?" I asked Belle.

"Oh yes. She was as gentle a soul as ever lived. Mother and Julia get their sweetness from her."

"Grandpa must not have got much of anything from her."

"Listen, little man, whatever your grandfather is or isn't can be blamed entirely upon the illustrious Oliver Spencer Kane."

"Why's that?"

She started to answer, then reconsidered. The mocking smile returned. She reached for my hands and began examining my palms and fingers. "Nice slender bone structure. I would say these hands were made to play piano, Thomas Kane."

I jerked away. "These hands were made to play basketball. Pianos are for women."

"Oh now, there are plenty of men who play."

"Yeah, like Liver-Archie. No thanks!"

Belle turned back to the piano with a sigh. "You are a typical Kane, I'll say that."

"How so?"

"Totally uncultured, and determined to stay that way. I can remember trying to interest your father in the piano when he was about your age. One would have thought I was introducing him to the black arts the way he avoided me after that. Such a pitiful group I was born into."

She began playing again.

"What's that song called?" I asked after a while.

"That song, as you refer to it, is 'Clair de Lune.' It was Grandmother's favorite. Do you like it?"

"It's okay, I guess."

"Your enthusiasm is a joy to behold. Do I dare assume there is some other piece you would rather hear?"

"How about 'Runaway'?"

"What in Heaven's name is 'Runaway'?"

"It's by Del Shannon. You know, the guy who hits all them high notes."

"Let's hear your second choice," she said.

"Okay. Uh, how about something by the Everly Brothers—'Cathy's Clown' or 'Bye Bye, Love.'"

"Sorry, kiddo. I'm afraid I've led too sheltered a life to have heard of Mr. Shannon or the Whateverly Brothers. No doubt they are part of that rock 'n' roll business."

"You got it."

"Well, I'll stick with Debussy if you don't mind."

She continued playing. Her fingers now moved across the keys as lightly as Julia's featherduster across the antique glassware. I would never have admitted it, but the music had a certain soothing effect. Just as I was beginning to relax, she stopped in the middle of a bar and spun around to face me as if I had called her a dirty name.

"Has the Chief told you what the big meeting is all about?"

"Huh?"

"The meeting, the meeting . . . You know what I'm talking about."

"No, I don't." She might as well have been asking me to name the stars in the Andromeda Galaxy.

"You expect me to believe that Junior never mentioned anything about coming down here for a pow-wow with the Chief?"

"I don't know a thing about any meeting. I just thought we came down for a visit."

She laughed as if I were the world's most naive inhabitant. Her eyes were wild. She looked the slightest bit loony.

"Your father does not just drop in when it pleases him, little fool. He comes when the Chief says to come, and that's all. The only reason you are here is because the Chief made a mysterious announcement a few weeks ago saying he wanted the whole family together for some unknown purpose. Your dad came running, just like he did a couple years back when the Chief gave him that old Buick."

"We got the Buick from the Chief?"

"Of course. The Most High said, 'Let there be transportation,' and there was transportation. A little gift every once in a while helps keep an outcast on a string."

"Why is Dad an outcast?"

"Oh, it's hard to remember exactly. He probably sneezed on a Sunday, or something like that. And there is the unforgettable fact that he's your grandfather's son."

"Will Grandpa be at this meeting?"

"I'm afraid he is not considered to be part of this family."

"Because of yesterday?"

"No . . . It's something which happened before either of us was born.".

"Tell me."

She shook her head. "You'll have to find that out from some-body else. I don't dare get on the Chief's blacklist this close to the big announcement. If it turns out to be what I think it is, I'll need to be on my best behavior or else my slice of the pie might get eaten away."

"What pie?" All I seemed to do was ask questions.

She laughed again, a strange, hollow laughter.

"What must it be like to be so innocent? I'm referring to the Kane inheritance and its distribution among surviving relatives. The Chief won't live forever, although it seems he already has. When he dies, it stands to reason that a few people's ships are going to come in. I just hope mine's as big as the *Queen Mary*."

"Or maybe the *Titanic*."

This time she didn't laugh. "I've already done my time on the bottom, kiddo. Too many years I rotted in this place under his thumb. I took off once, with a good-looking character in an Oldsmobile, but that didn't last long. We had some high times, but he didn't look nearly so good after the money ran out. I ended up back here getting the third degree from everybody in the family. But they never found out anything, and they never will. Since then I've just been marking time. When that old fool dies, I'll start to live. Until then I play the game."

She turned away from me and began softly playing a variation of a simple tune I hadn't heard since second grade. In a husky, somewhat sinister-sounding voice she sang:

> *This old fool, he play seven,*
> *He play knickknack up in heaven.*
> *Knickknack paddywhack, give a dog a bone,*
> *This old fool went rolling home.*

The upright hairs on my arms and neck told me it was time to leave. I backed out of the parlor feeling like a participant in some horror movie. The half-mad woman at the piano, creating the eerie music, was merely a supporting player in the confused melodrama. As usual, I had no understanding of the plot or what part I would be expected to play.

MISSOURI

*E*arly Wednesday morning, every cloud in the Western Hemisphere seemed to be unloading its contents over Climer. I awoke to a chilled bedroom with nothing covering me but dime-store underwear and a layer of goosebumps, thanks to Fred who had the entire sheet and bedspread wrapped tightly around him. His head and feet stuck out opposite ends of the roll like a hotdog protruding from a bun. I gave the pile a stiff yank.

"Gimme some covers, you hog."

My effort caused a reverse window shade effect that sent Fred unraveling toward the side of the bed. He gained consciousness just in time to scream and make a desperate grab for the brass post at the head of the frame. For a moment he teetered on the edge of the cliff, then inched backward to safety. I was afraid his cry of alarm would bring our parents into the room, but the din of wind-driven rain smacking the side of the hotel was too much even for Fred's mouth to overcome.

"I'm telling," he said, struggling to regain his rightful three-quarters of the covers.

I knew by the vacant look in his eyes that he wasn't going to do anything other than fall back asleep. Which he did. I was content to lay beside him, listening to the wind rattle the windowpanes. Outside, the ancient oak slapped its branches against the glass, as if begging to enter the hotel until the storm passed. I pulled a corner of the spread up under my chin.

After a while I smelled bacon frying; Julia and Inez were

already on the job. I wondered what it must be like to be an old lady, doing nothing but cooking and cleaning all the time. Did they ever get tired of it? Did they ever long to kick off their shoes and just run through soft grass on a sunny afternoon? Did they know, or even care, that Roger Maris and Mickey Mantle hit home runs for the Yankees yesterday? Probably not.

All things considered, it was hard to fault old ladies for latching on to religion when the opportunity arose. They certainly didn't have much else going for them. At least that's the way I saw it. What didn't make any sense at all was getting religion at a young age, like the Chief said he had done. Surely there were better ways to occupy one's days. Even in boring McKinley, Iowa a guy would rather play catch with Hippo than sing hymns and wear black clothes all the time.

In the Chief's defense, maybe the old days were so boring that even religion looked good. On the other hand, how dull could it have been killing Indians and exploring new frontiers? As usual, the whole business of God and religion left me spinning in all directions. I gave up, and went downstairs to see if one of the aunts might slip me a piece of bacon before breakfast.

I had never witnessed the hotel's early-morning routine. Julia was busy setting the table. I found Inez in the kitchen, tending two large, black skillets. A mound of bacon covered an oversized platter on the counter. I gave her my most pitiful look and received one of the hot, crispy strips in return.

"You're up early this morning," she said cheerily.

"The rain woke me up."

"Well, shame on it then. I guess rain does have a way of messing up a little boy's day, doesn't it, Tommy."

"I don't know. I'll ask Fred sometime."

She caught my meaning and laughed. Then Belle passed through the kitchen, headed for the bathroom. She hadn't had time to work on her face, that was obvious. I wished she had waited until this morning to ask me to guess her age.

Half an hour later, the dining room chairs were full and everything was as it should be, except for the rain. It continued falling, as if some celestial angel of maintenance had forgotten to shut off the spigot. What was I going to do all day if the skies didn't clear?

The solution to my problem came from an unexpected source. In the middle of a bite of jellied toast, the Chief suddenly informed everyone of what a fine job I had done as cemetery grounds-keeper. Nearly forty-eight hours had passed since I completed the work. He hadn't said a word one way or the other, although the money had been left on the vanity in our bedroom. The method of payment made it easy to assume that he had not been pleased. Now he was praising me. All eyes were looking my way, and I tried to remain humble.

"I've got another job for you, Thomas Jamison," the Chief said.

"What's that?"

"I want you to check out the attic for leaks in the roof. We don't get rains like this too often, but when we do it's a good time to see if we're watertight. There's a lot of clutter up there, but I'm sure you can maneuver through it and make a thorough inspection. Understand?"

"Yes, sir. How much do you pay?"

I was only halfway serious about the money, but he was completely unamused.

"I don't pay one red cent! The day I have to give a youngster money to check the roof over his own head will be a sorry one for both of us. If you are too lazy to do the job, I'll take care of it myself."

All eyes were still looking my way, and I tried not to melt to the floor in shame. Belle was smiling as she sipped her orange juice.

"I'll go up," I told the Chief. "I was just making a joke."

He took a vicious bite of toast, refusing to answer me or even look my way. The rest of the meal was eaten in silence, except for the scraping of forks against plates and the drumming of the rain.

• • • •

The third-floor attic was cavernous. I made a slow sweep of the darkened spaces in front of me with my flashlight. The thin, yellow beam reached about ten feet into the black, then faded, as if it dared go no farther. Every sort of shadow danced beyond the faint light. I found myself nervous at the prospect of advancing into the unknown without a greater source of illumination. Who could guess what might lurk in the hidden places of the old hotel?

An explosion of thunder moistened my palms. I swung around, shining my light along the wall. Just inside the doorway was an electrical switch. With the mere flick of a finger, mouth-drying shapes were rendered harmless and replaced by an intriguing collection of junk that demanded immediate inspection.

Knocking down a tattered cobweb, I saw that one section of the upper floor had been reserved for dying furniture. Overstuffed sofas, their insides exposed and hanging out, sat dust-covered, mortally wounded. A dozen or more wooden chairs, suffering amputated legs or broken backs, were piled on top of a headless bed.

Beyond these were stacks of old magazines decorated with spider's lace and smelling of mildew. Behind the magazines were dozens of crates and boxes jammed full of seemingly unrelated items. The first one I emptied contained Thanksgiving decorations, a lamp shade, one green rubber boot, the head of a rake, and two packages of dominoes. Another box, marked "train," held a wonderful electric model of a Union Pacific passenger train. The bullet-shaped engine had a Christmas tree bulb in place of the original headlight. I was curious to know if it worked, but I had given up playing with toys. Reluctantly I repacked the box and continued my exploration.

For another hour I dug through drawers, crates, and trunks looking for whatever treasures one might discover in an attic in Climer, Missouri. Every few minutes I checked the ceiling for leaks. There was no water to be found, but something else caught my attention. Inside a leather trunk marked "Lathom Kane" was a ragged, black diary. Its red pages had faded to an ugly orange. Some of them were stuck together, and whole sections had pulled away from the binding. A random reading of the entries showed nothing of interest until the words "old silver" jumped at me. On September the sixteenth of some unspecified year, the author had written, "Today I buried the last of the old silver behind the tower. Fifty paces off the point of the back left corner. If I leave it in the house while I'm in the hospital it will be gone by the time I get back. Myra won't like this."

I turned the page, anxious for more information, but the rest of the diary was blank. Rereading the passage made my pulse rate climb. Was it possible I had stumbled onto something wonderful, or was my imagination running wild? Old silver! The words conjured up visions of rotted sacks bursting with gleaming silver coins, or buried caches of bullion bars and intricately-etched jewelry. But who was Lathom Kane, and where was the tower he had used as a reference point? Had anyone else read his diary, or was I the first to learn his secret?

I had to find the answers to those questions, and had to do so in a manner which would not arouse suspicion. Belle or the Chief could probably supply any information I needed, but they would want to ask more questions than they answered. Other sources would better serve my purpose. I returned the diary to the bottom of the leather trunk and headed downstairs to probe the minds of Julia and Inez.

• • • •

The storm had passed; the sky was showing expanding patches of blue. Robins hopped about in the yard, pulling worms from the damp grass. I found Julia and Inez sitting in an oversized porch swing, talking quietly. The porch floorboards creaked with each step I took, but the aunts failed to notice. I didn't want to break up their conversation, nor appear to be an eavesdropper. I coughed and cleared my throat like a wino at daybreak.

Julia looked over the top of her glasses.

"Well, here's a handsome young lad come to visit his old aunties. Come sit." She patted the space in the swing between herself and Inez.

"I didn't mean to interrupt."

"Fiddlesticks," said Inez, "we would much rather talk to you than with each other. We bore ourselves to death rehashing all the stale gossip."

"Absolutely," agreed Julia. "Now, what is on your mind?"

Thoughts of old silver were on my mind, but I pushed them aside to concentrate on saying the right words. It wasn't easy.

"Who is Lathom Kane?"

"Well now, let's see," Julia said. "He was Poppa's brother's son, which makes him our first cousin, which would make him your, uh . . ."

"It makes him your distant relation," said Inez.

"Did he live around here?"

Julia nodded. "Yes . . . He had a shack just off Hollingsworth Road, about a quarter-mile out of town. They tore it down, of course, when the turkey farm began operating."

"Turkey farm?"

"National Poultry Incorporated, Climer's largest industry. There must be seven or eight men working during the busy season. Wouldn't you say so, sister?"

"I would," said Inez, snapping off a strand of thread with her teeth as she finished sewing the pocket of a brown dress. "There is talk of expansion too."

I was amused and touched by their hometown pride. The aunts were as innocent as a kindergarten kiss. But this was no time for sentiment.

"What ever happened to Lathom Kane?

"He died, poor man. I don't remember now what from, but he lived a hard life and it finally caught up to him. He ran around with your grandfather for years. Those two used to spend half their time in saloons and the other half recovering. Toward the end Lathom got to looking all dried-up and yellow. They finally took him to the hospital, and the good Lord never saw fit to let him come out alive. Poor man."

"Poppa says a man begins to die the moment he first takes alcohol into his mouth," said Julia. "Lathom was a perfect example . . . So many wasted years. And I'm afraid our brother is not much different."

The clock inside the hotel struck 11.

"Oh my," said Julia, popping up, "where does the time go? I've got to peel potatoes and start the roast."

"I'll be right with you, dear, as soon as I sew this button," promised Inez.

I followed Julia as she marched toward the kitchen. It was surprising how swiftly those short, heavy legs could move when duty called. I struggled to stay close.

"I don't suppose he had much money."

"Who is that, Thomas?"

"Lathom Kane."

"Oh no . . . I doubt it. He drank away any money he had. The shack he lived in wasn't fit for cattle . . . How his wife put up with it, I'll never know. Myra wasn't much better than him, though, when push came to shove. She drank too much herself, and that didn't help Lathom any."

"Did he work someplace?"

"He tried, but he was always so frail. About the only thing he seemed to have a talent for was gambling, and that is certainly no way to make a living."

Gambling! Again the image of silver coins entered my mind. I could see sprawling piles of round dollars being raked in at the fortuitous turning of an ace or king. My heart was off to the races once more. But before I could continue the questioning, the Chief came into the kitchen to ask me about leaks in the roof. The only leaks concerning me at the moment were informational leaks regarding the treasure. I got away from him as soon as possible and went to Inez for one last question. As she pushed her needle through buttonholes, she provided me with directions to National Poultry Incorporated. After dinner I would begin the search for old silver!

• • • •

The turkey farm was not a pretty sight. Fourteen long wooden buildings, speckled with random patches of tar paper and corrugated tin, were divided into two rows of seven by a muddy drive. Wire fencing enclosed roosting pens, and the terrain inside them resembled the desolate surface of the moon. White feathers coated the buildings, the fences, and the ground. They floated around me like gigantic, curved snowflakes. Their color made me wonder if the aunts had confused turkeys with chickens.

The air was full of more than just feathers. Smells which could never have been properly described in polite company moved past my nose with brazen nonchalance. My eyes began to water.

"Hey, boy! . . . What's your business here?"

A bare-chested man in green work pants walked toward me. He was shorter than me, but his diameter was twice my own. His deeply-tanned stomach was massive, swaying left or right with every step. Had it been any larger, he would have needed a wheel or some other means of support to avoid toppling over. His skin glistened with sweat. Individual droplets hung precariously from strands of the coarse, black hair matting his upper body.

"I'm looking for a job," I said.

He laughed in my face, and I saw that his teeth had known hard times.

"This ain't a babysittin' outfit I run here, boy. I need men to work these birds. You better stick to scoopin' ice cream or mowin' somebody's grass."

"I'm stronger than I look."

"You'd have to be. I seen more muscles on a garden hose."

He was ready to walk away. I was desperate to keep him talking.

"I gotta work here a few days, mister, and the money's not that important. I'd settle for half-pay if you would just give me a chance."

"Well, lookee here now, boy, you ain't makin' much sense to me. You say it's real important to get work, then you say the money don't make no difference. I say maybe you don't know up from down, an' it might be a good idea to haul your sorry carcass back to wherever it was you came from."

He waited for me to leave. It was time to take a chance.

"I'm staying at the Kane Hotel in case you change your mind."

"Why you stayin' there?"

"My family is here for a visit. Chief Kane is my great-grandfather."

"Chief Kane your great-granddaddy?" The man spoke in tones of near-reverence.

"That's right. He said it might help to mention his name." I figured one small lie couldn't be held against a kid trying to find old silver.

"Help? Why, when somebody speaks Chief Kane's name around these parts, it's almost like they was usin' the name of President Harry Truman hisself. Course, he ain't president no more, but I think you get my drift."

"I get it."

The man threw his arm across my shoulder. Incredible as it

seemed, the odor from his armpit made me forget the other smells that were polluting the air around me.

"Don't you worry about nothin'," he said. "You can work as long as you want an' quit when you gotta quit. Full wages too. An' don't worry about the work bein' too hard because ol' Bob's gonna take good care of you. Say, I didn't catch the name."

"Tom Kane."

He stuck out his hand. "I'm Bob C. Ricketts, but folks call me Cricketts on account of stickin' my middle initial up next to my last name. Now, when did you want to start, Tom?"

"How about now?"

He slapped my back, nearly shattering the shoulder blade.

"By golly, boy, if you ain't a chip off the old block. That's just the way Chief Kane operates; everything's right now. None of that tomorrow stuff for him, nosiree. But the fact is, I need to fill out papers an' all before I can work a man. How about we take a look-see around the place an' then start off fresh in the mornin'.'"

"Fine with me."

"Attaboy."

We walked farther down the twin rows of buildings. The roosting pens overflowed with squawking, scratching, pecking masses of white birds. The ugly creatures didn't appear too intelligent, but I could never have guessed how dumb they really were.

"Ever worked a poultry farm before, Tom?"

"No."

"Then you're in for a real experience. Ain't nothin' else like it."

Cricketts led me to a dilapidated brick building with a collapsed rear wall. The strange structure resembled a bombed-out church. We stepped through the frame of a rotted screen door onto a wooden floor that was coated with a quarter-inch of dried pigeon droppings. There was no light except what filtered through twisted rafters and dangling debris where the wall had fallen. A flight of damp cement stairs led us to a basement that Pueblo Indian cliff-dwellers would have considered primitive. With one dim bulb standing between us and midnight, I strained to see the obscure figures occupying the corners of the dungeon.

"Got a new man here," the boss said to the denizens of that underground world. A thick silence made it clear that no one cared about meeting a new worker. "He's gonna be with us a few days while he's visitin' his Great-Granddaddy Kane over at the hotel."

My eyes were growing accustomed to the lack of light, and the shadowy forms took on detail. Dark ovals became faces, and I understood by the expressions upon them that being related to the Chief would do me little, if any, good in this group.

Cricketts started introducing the other workers to me.

"Now this fellah here is Massachusetts Rodgers, an' that happy-lookin' character is ol' Spriggs, an' the guy—"

"Hey, Cricketts," yelled a voice at the top of the stairs.

"Yeah?"

"Telephone. Long distance from St. Loo."

"Well, if that don't figure. You boys will have to finish introducin' yourselves to young Kane here. Catch you later."

With surprising agility, Bob C. Ricketts bounded up the stairs two at a time, leaving me among strangers.

I could see them clearly now, and what I saw wasn't too encouraging. Sitting on a wooden folding chair was a man whose clothes would have shamed a Depression bum. His shirt looked as if it had been run through a lawnmower; the pants he wore were smitten with advanced leprosy. A cigarette with an inch-long ash hung from his mouth, and his chin rested upon his chest. I would have thought he was sleeping except that his eyes were open and unblinking. Maybe he was dead and nobody had noticed.

On a bench along the opposite wall sat a younger man with high cheekbones and greased-back hair. He sneered at me in a manner indicating we were already enemies.

"I ain't no fan of your Chief Kane," he said.

"Is that a fact?"

"You bet it is, sonny. He tossed my old man off the Fire Department years back just for getting a snootful and bumping the truck into a tree. It broke my old man's heart, and he ain't never lived it down."

The third man in the group, sitting cross-legged on the floor beside a small hole, laughed uproariously. He wore bib overalls, a green shirt, and a striped engineer cap. I guessed him to be about sixty.

"Don't pay no attention to him, kid," he said. "He's goofy as a fly in a Jack Daniels bottle. Only thing that ever broke his daddy's heart was havin' a son that growed up to be a idjit."

"You shut your face, Massachusetts," screamed the younger man, "or I'll tear your tongue out by the roots!"

Massachusetts Rodgers, as the boss had called him, laughed even louder at the threat, then spit a stream of tobacco juice at the hole in the floor.

"Don Books is like one of them Mexican Chewowwow dogs," he said, wiping his chin on the knee of his overalls. "He makes lotsa noise, but after ya get a good look at him ya just gotta laugh yer guts out."

I barely avoided a collision with the one called Don Books as he brushed past me and stomped up the slimy stairs. He stopped at the top to profane everyone in the basement and make bizarre threats against our anatomies. His talk made me somewhat nervous, but Massachusetts continued to laugh and spit. The silent, raggedy man showed no sign of life, let alone concern. It was becoming obvious to me that all the turkeys were not necessarily confined to the roosting pens.

Books finally left the building. Massachusetts dug into a wrinkled tobacco pouch and inserted a brown wad behind his lower lip. Water from a leaky faucet dripped noisily into a grimy sink. A *kamikaze* fly dive-bombed the light bulb, as if its sole reason for existing was to plunge us into darkness.

"Chaw?" offered Massachusetts.

"No thanks."

He returned the pouch to his pocket and struggled to his feet. "Name's Massachusetts Conlon Rodgers."

"Tom Kane."

He took a couple more shots at the hole in the floor. His aim left much to be desired.

"You must be from Massachusetts," I said, trying not to stare at the brown puddles he created.

"Never been near the place."

"Then how come you're named Massachusetts?"

"Because my mammy couldn't spell Ohio." The comatose man in rags made a strangled, wheezing sound that got Massachusetts excited. "Mark it down on yer calendar, kid—I almost got ol'

Spriggsy to laugh just now. That old buzzard hasn't done nothin'
but frown an' pout in the two years I knowed him, but by golly if
he didn't almost cut loose just now. How did it feel, Spriggsy old
boy?"

Spriggs moved his mournful eyes from Massachusetts to me,
then stood and walked rigidly up the stairs.

"I think you made him mad," I said to Massachusetts.

"Nah, he just gets a little spooky with so much talkin' goin' on.
He'll work like a plowhorse all day long, but he ain't much good at
words. Course, that ain't no problem because me an' bigmouth
Books talk enough to take up slack."

"That Books guy looks like a weirdo to me."

"That's cuz he is. All of us here is a little cracked, else we
wouldn't be stayin' around. An' that makes me wonder why a rel-
ative of a bigshot like Chief Kane would be sniffin' around a dump
like this."

"Oh, I just want to earn some money to make up for what I lost
the other day at the carnival over in Hadleyville."

"Get cleaned out, did ya?"

"Completely. Dropped about thirty bucks."

"Whooee! I can see old Massachusetts is gonna have to teach
you a few things about life. I put in sixty-one years worth, so I
know the ropes pretty good. Ain't got no bucks, but I got experience an' that's a lot better. Let's get some air."

We left the fetid silence of the basement for the tumultuous
stench outside. Massachusetts showed me the rest of the setup,
promising to be available the next morning to help me get started.
We shook hands, then I returned to the hotel feeling quite pleased
with myself. Step One had been a success. Tomorrow I would begin
a cautious, calculated investigation of the turkey farm. Somewhere
among its collection of fowls and fools were the answers I needed
to find Lathom Kane's old silver.

MISSOURI

6

*T*hursday morning was a time of announcements. The Chief went first.

"I won't be home for the evening meal, but I'll want to meet with all of you right back here in this room tonight at 7:30 sharp! The issue is of extreme importance to each of you, so let's not have any stragglers."

Nobody said anything for a while, but curious glances were exchanged across the table. Belle gave Dad a confident wink; this was obviously what she had been talking to me about the other day in the parlor. He nodded vacantly and resumed eating. I took advantage of the lengthy silence to inform everyone of my job at the turkey farm.

I had purposely delayed mentioning it to cut down the amount of reaction time my parents would have. A quick answer was less likely to be negative. Unfortunately, the tactic was ineffective.

"Where did you come up with an ignorant idea like that?" asked Dad.

"What's wrong with it?"

"It's idiotic. We brought you down here to visit relatives, not to work on a farm with a bunch of stinking turkeys."

"You're too young for something like this, Tommy," said Mom.

"Yeah," Dad added, "just forget that whole business."

I almost got sick. My plan for getting inside the farm had worked out beautifully, but I wasn't being allowed to proceed to Step Two. Would I have to reveal my secret, old silver and all?

"I think he should be allowed to work," the Chief said. "A little hard labor is good for a boy, and it will help him make up some of the money he squandered the other day. Junior, I say let him do it. It may help him learn the value of a dollar."

Dad wasn't about to argue, especially on the day of the big announcement. So he made a complete reversal, parroting exactly what the Chief said as if he had just then thought of it himself. But wrinkles on Mom's forehead caught my attention. Wrinkles signaled worry and uncertainty. I excused myself from the table before she could muster a protest.

"Don't work too hard, Thomas Jamison," the Chief called after me, "and don't be late tonight. Remember . . . 7:30 . . . sharp."

• • • •

Once again I descended into the basement of the partially-collapsed brick building. Turkey farm workers seemed to congregate under that structure like cockroaches under a floor-drain grate. It wouldn't have surprised me to see some of them sprouting antennae.

Massachusetts Conlon Rodgers was trying to lure Cricketts into a bet.

"No guts," he taunted.

"Now doggone it, don't rush me," Cricketts said. "I got to get this straight in my mind first. You're sayin' I get to cut the deck three times for a quarter, an' if I don't hit a ace, a deuce, or a one-eyed jack I win?"

Massachusetts shuffled a deck of cards with hunting dogs pictured on the backside. His cigar smelled like a burning mattress.

"That's the deal. I say there ain't a man alive who can make three cuts without hittin' aces, deuces, or one-eyed johnnies. An' I'm puttin' my money where my mouth is."

Cricketts calculated on his fingers and concluded Massachusetts was wrong. "I'm in for a quarter's worth."

"What about you, motormouth?" Massachusetts asked Don Books.

"The only cuts I'm interested in are across your throat," Books said.

"How about you, Spriggsy?" Spriggs, wearing the same shamble of clothes as the day before, shook his head no. Massachusetts looked at me. "I'd ask ya in, kid, but I don't take from them who just got fleeced by carnival gypsies."

"Quit talkin' an' lay them cards down," said Cricketts.

Massachusetts gave the deck one last riffle, then set it on top of the wooden bench where everyone had gathered. The boss popped his fingers for luck and made the first cut. It was the four of spades.

"Attababy!" he yelled.

The second cut produced the ten of diamonds. Cricketts's confidence soared. "One more time an' you're a goner, Massachusetts."

Massachusetts shrugged. "A dance ain't over till they play 'Good Night Ladies.'"

Cricketts knocked on wood, blew up his sleeve, and called out to a couple of Patron Saints before making the final cut. With great dramatization he put a thick hand over the deck and separated it two-thirds of the way down. After a deep breath, he flicked his wrist to reveal the ace of spades.

"Of all the stinkin' luck," he muttered, tossing the cards onto the bench.

"No luck about it," grinned Massachusetts. "Ain't a man alive can do it."

Cricketts dug through his pockets for another quarter. Don Books stepped in front of him to slam a dollar against the wood.

"Feel like covering that, old man?"

"Yer covered."

Don Books took the deck and shuffled for what seemed like nine days.

"C'mon, man," Massachusetts muttered, "we'll all be dead before you make the first cut."

"Just don't want you stacking the deck, that's all."

"Mother Nature already stacked the deck against you, boy," said Massachusetts.

Books clenched his jaws, but made no reply. He cut the deck, turning up the jack of spades. Massachusetts chuckled and pocketed the dollar.

"No man alive can do it," he said. "No idjit neither."

Books took the card that had made him a loser and tore the top off with his teeth. "That's your head, Rodgers," he snarled, spitting a spade to the floor.

Cricketts jerked his arm. "You better cool off, boy. I told you before that we ain't got room on this farm for no locos. You go ahead an' take young Kane over to get started on number 12. An' don't be showin' him none of your crazy fits."

"I sorta promised the kid I'd show him the ropes, Cricketts," Massachusetts said.

"No you don't," Cricketts said, laying down another quarter. "We got a few more of these games to get played. Books can take care of it okay."

The last person I wanted to spend time with, on a turkey farm or anyplace else, was Don Books. Massachusetts liked to say that Books had a few of his pages torn out at birth. The guy belonged in a padded cell. He always had a faraway look on his face, much like Tony Perkins in *Psycho*. Nothing less than the lure of old silver could have made me follow him to shed number 12.

Our first task was opening the numerous doors leading out to the roosting pen. After hooking the last one into place, Books stepped inside shed 12. I did likewise, and my fever for old silver was instantly chilled. The smell was so bad, it made my nose run. Dust was a dirty finger reaching down my throat. All I could see were waves and waves of necks and heads screeching to be watered and fed. The noise and stench overwhelmed me. I backed outside, coughing heavily.

"Can't take it huh, punk," smirked Books. He took deep breaths of the rancid air to show how unaffected he was by the atmosphere that had forced my retreat.

"I'll be all right in a second."

"Ahhh, you ain't even worth taking the time to train. If you weren't Chief Kane's relation you wouldn't have got a foot inside the gate, and we both know it. Get your tail back in here right now, or I'll tell Cricketts you ran into my fist with your front teeth."

I might have been more afraid of the guy if I didn't already despise him so much. I had to show him I could take anything this place had to offer.

My second entry into the shed was slightly easier. The worst of the putrid air had seeped out through the opened doors, and rapidly draining sinuses filtered most of what remained. Dust and head-throbbing noise still swirled about me, but I knew I wouldn't have to step outside again. At least not for a while.

Sweat droplets jumped from my pores as I followed Don Books into a storage room at the end of the shed. He lifted a fifty-pound sack of pellet feed and threw it at me.

"Fill them feeders."

The feeders were nothing more than tin troughs suspended from the ceiling by chains. I struggled to get the awkward sack up to my chest. Turkeys, already massed around my feet in a feeding frenzy, threatened to engulf me in a feathery whirlpool. There was no place to move without putting a foot on some bird's back. I didn't know what to do, and Books loved it.

"You got to be smarter than the turkeys," he sneered. "Watch how it's done, punk."

He began swinging his legs from the hips, knees locked, in the manner of a Nazi foot soldier. With obvious relish, he rammed his boots into the wall of birds sending them sailing and screeching in every direction. Noise and dust levels rose nearly beyond human tolerance as Books proudly demonstrated his prowess at crowd dispersal. Just when I thought a choice would have to be made between another embarrassing exit or suffocation, he stopped.

"See, any idiot can do it."

"Obviously."

After a few false starts, I adopted a gentler form of his technique. Instead of kicking, I slid my feet along the floor and sort of scooped the ravenous creatures out of the way. The feeding went reasonably well from that point onward. Then Books showed me what came next.

"Time to move everybody outside," he said. "These birds need fresh air, but sometimes they try to stay indoors. Know what happens then?"

"No."

"This."

Again he kicked turkeys like a man possessed. Birds flew out the doors, end over end, into the roosting-pen dirt. A few of the more intelligent ones left of their own accord, but most were content to wait for him to leave his footprint beneath their tail feathers.

He seemed capable of continuing the effort indefinitely, and might have done so if one of the airborne birds hadn't missed the door. The unfortunate turkey ricocheted off the door casing and somersaulted back toward Books. It slid down his back, sharp claws tearing his shirt like a paper bag. Books went berserk.

"You filthy vulture," he screamed, "I'll have your head for that!"

I watched dumbfounded as he grabbed the turkey by the neck, punched it senseless, and hurled it to the floor.

"Try something now, baby," he dared.

The battered bird lay deathly still; its purple tongue hung out the side of its beak. Nearby turkeys cocked their heads in curiosity to examine a fallen comrade.

For a second I thought the incident was over. But as the conqueror turned away, the foolish victim tried to get up. Books pounced like a starving tiger.

"Second-time offenders get the death penalty in this state."

With that decree, he proceeded to drag the doomed bird to the storage room.

"You're not really going to kill that thing, are you?" I asked him.

"Got to. If one of these birds steps out of line and don't pay the price, the whole shed could go bad."

His sweating face was streaked with dirt and slop from the floor. He giggled like a lunatic while bending down behind a pile of empty feed sacks. I watched him uncover a red tobacco can filled with firecrackers. Strange how firecrackers kept turning up everywhere I went.

"Eat this," he said, pulling one from the can and jamming it into the turkey's mouth. A twine from one of the sacks was used to tie the beak shut. The bird appeared to be smoking a striped cigar.

"This doesn't make sense," I said. "You can't teach turkeys anything by killing one of them."

"No mercy," he said through gritted teeth. "Sinners die."

Books stuck his knee into the bird's back and lit a match. The fuse sparked. I barely got my ears plugged before the firecracker decapitated the turkey. Stale air inside the storage room was immediately filled with the acrid smell of spent nitrate and singed feathers.

The headless bird thrashed along the floor, then achieved flight. It traveled upside down, bouncing off the ceiling and walls. Blood spewed from its neck like rusty water from some grotesque garden hose. A horrible sucking sound could be heard.

Don Books breathed like a man with holes in his lungs. His eyes were golfballs. As the bloody bird shot past him, flipping some of the warm red liquid onto his cheek and forehead, he recoiled in horror.

"Sinner's blood," he moaned, "can't ever be washed away."

He beat his fists against the wall and began to sob.

I had seen enough. I ran out the door, right past a startled Massachusetts Conlon Rodgers.

"Slow down a little," he called after me, "you're makin' the rest of us look bad."

I didn't bother to answer, and I didn't slow down.

• • • •

It was peaceful in the little cemetery. Surrounded by sunflower walls, I felt as if the rest of the world had evaporated and floated away. Except for the distant chugging of a tractor, there were no human-produced sounds to be heard. A group of white butterflies sat atop the grave of Eleanor Kane, slowly fanning their wings as if to keep her resting-place cool. Cardinals flitted among the giant flower heads, their brilliant reds contrasting with the pale yellow petals.

The solitude was a balm to my confused mind. The wild palpitations of my heart, brought on by the bizarre incident at the turkey farm, diminished as I lay in the warm grass. Was Don Books crazy or what? Normal people didn't go around blowing up turkeys and screaming about "sinner's blood." That was almost as bad as the preacher I saw on television who said he had been washed in the blood of a lamb. These types should not be running loose.

A guy like Books was capable of anything, and he had just shot a gaping hole in my plans for finding the old silver. How could I do any investigating with that misfit around? He wasn't safe under any circumstances, and taking my eyes off him while treasure hunting could prove fatal. If I ended up dead, the old silver wouldn't do me any more good than it was doing Lathom Kane.

A marauding bee rousted me from my bed in the grass. I took a fast lap around the cemetery until the intruder drifted off in search of slower prey. Momentum carried me to a spot near the grave of Paul Jamison Kane. I was reminded of my first visit to this place, and of the Chief's talk about God. Nothing had happened since then to help me decide whether or not to believe. The issue was too complicated.

A seed of logic sprouted inside my skull. If God was a lie, yet a guy still believed, what could it hurt? But if God was real, and a guy didn't believe, it could be bad news. I decided to play it safe and believe, although I wasn't sure I believed even after the decision was made. Maybe a guy should ask for a sign or something.

After further deliberation, I concluded that seeking a sign would not be out of line. I had no idea how to go about communicating with God, but there was no doubt as to what my terms would be. For lack of anything more sophisticated, I knelt down and mumbled, "Show me how to get the old silver and I'll know You're real."

I waited for the skies to part or the earth to open. Nothing happened. A lightning bolt would have been acceptable, or even a Scripture-quoting butterfly. A summer snowflake, red rain, anything at all would have been preferable to the unchanging silence pressing down from above. My infantile faith began to wither. I kicked at the ground, wondering how I could have been so stupid as to attempt to bargain with pie in the sky. Dad was right—there wasn't anything up there but blue space. It was time to leave.

As I passed the last headstone—Lathom Kane's headstone—I saw a reflection of something lying in the grass. A quarter was nestled amid the green blades. I stared at it a while, uncomprehending. It was merely a coin somebody had dropped, a plain everyday quarter with a 1956 minting date. I had already stuck it into my pocket when the truth hit me: this was the sign I had asked for! It had to be. Even the staunchest nonbeliever would be hard-pressed to dispute the finding of a silver coin near the grave of Lathom Kane just after asking God for a visible manifestation of His existence. The message was unmistakable, and I danced like a drunken sailor. All that buried silver would soon be mine, and I had God to thank. My faith grew like Jack's beanstalk. How had I ever doubted Him?

For several minutes I basked in the glow of paradise regained, but then the leering image of Don Books forced its way into my thoughts. I still didn't know what to do about him, or if I should even go back there at all. But how could I find the old silver if I didn't return to the scene of his murderous crime? I looked at the quarter. This was a simple question of yes or no; why not let God speak through the tool He gave me? I flipped the coin into the air. "Heads I go, tails I stay." With all the angels in Heaven as witnesses, God told me to return to the turkey farm. Who was I to disobey?

• • • •

Don Books sat atop a Minneapolis-Moline tractor, talking to Massachusetts Conlon Rodgers and Spriggs the Sphinx. Approaching them from the rear, I heard him bragging how he had run me off the place.

"I knew he wasn't going to be any good the first time I seen him. Soon as I made him do a little work, he hit the road. He's just a punk, and I don't care who his relation is."

Massachusetts juiced up the ground in front of the tractor tire he was leaning against.

"I figgered the kid might do better 'n that," he said. "Didn't strike me as the quittin' kind."

"He was just a punk," Books insisted.

I walked up behind Massachusetts and tapped his shoulder. He turned his neck rather than his body.

"What do we do next?" I asked as if nothing had happened.

"Well shut my mouth," he said. "We thought you flew the coop, kid."

Books glared at me in undisguised hatred.

"You ran out on me, you skinny punk, and I don't like that. You left me with all the work, and then you show up when we're on break. I ought to flatten your face!"

He didn't look as crazy now as inside the shed, but there was definitely something loose inside that head of his. He despised me even more than I did him, and he was much more capable of doing something about it. In a fight I would have little hope of winning. The sensible approach would be to outthink him.

"I had to run home a minute," I said.

"What for, to put your paper dolls to bed?"

"I forgot to take my medicine before I came to work."

"Medicine for what?"

"Uh . . . for a deviated septum." That was the only medical term I could think of. I learned it from watching The Three Stooges.

Don Books jumped off the tractor and stuck his chin in my face.

"I don't care anything about your diseases, punk. Just don't ever run out on me again. You get what I'm saying?"

"Sure."

He stared me down, then stomped off, walking with his arms away from his sides as if he had a watermelon under each one.

"Good riddance," Massachusetts said, shaking his head. "I think the doc musta slapped the wrong end when that idjit was hatched."

I was about to tell him what Books had done earlier when a dust cloud appeared at the far end of the grounds. We watched it move toward us. Cricketts's green pickup finally came around the far shed, sliding to a stop in front of our group. The cloud arrived shortly thereafter.

"Hop in, men," he yelled. "We got us a situation out on the range."

Spriggs, Massachusetts, and I crammed into the cab. We drove out the back gate. Seconds later a raunchy stink hit us, nearly causing my breakfast to land on the dashboard. It made the rest of the turkey farm smell like spice cake.

"She's ripe today," laughed Cricketts.

"What is it?" I gasped.

"Turkey heaven or turkey hell, whichever you prefer. It's where we put the dead ones that get hauled outta the sheds. We lose forty or fifty birds a day, an' they all end up over there eventually."

He pointed to a large, circular depression of dirt in the middle of a nearby field. The surface of the dirt was noticeably lower than the surrounding grassland, and very uneven. It all looked innocent enough, but, oh, the vile fumes!

"Who does the burying?" I asked.

"Each man takes care of his own dead," Cricketts said. "That's the only fair way to handle it."

I knew right then that no turkey had better die inside my sheds because nothing could make me go near such a terrible place. Absolutely, positively nothing.

• • • •

The "range" was sixty acres of fenced ground which provided the space necessary to raise turkeys that had outgrown the roosting pens. The "situation" Cricketts had mentioned was a couple hundred escaped birds scattered across the countryside. They had managed to knock down a section of fence, and now occupied the branches of every bush and small tree in the vicinity. Some strutted the ditches of a gravel road; a few perched on a rusted plow just beyond the range boundary.

"Let's spread out an' herd 'em all back to the busted fence," Cricketts said.

Moving quickly but cautiously so as not to stampede the escapees, we extended ourselves to the edge of their migration. I grabbed one turkey by the feet and had another on the run when a distant whistle touched my eardrums, even above the squawking and flapping. I saw Massachusetts frantically waving his arms, pointing to something behind him.

"C'mon, Tom," Cricketts yelled over to me.

It took me about ten seconds to catch and pass the boss; he moved with all the swiftness of a glacier. Massachusetts disappeared behind a grassy knoll. I sprinted to the top and got a good look at the problem. A set of railroad tracks curved across the land below me. For nearly a quarter-mile the rails were dotted with turkeys. A small circle of light was visible on the horizon. I knew it would only be a minute or two until a sleek high-speed passenger train, the Kansas City Flyer, would make its daily slash across Pettis County.

Massachusetts and I reached the tracks at the same time. He

headed left; I went to the right, toward the train. It was already obvious to me that many birds were going to get creamed if they didn't move on their own.

Reaching the the closest turkey, I gave a breathless kick and watched it flutter about a yard off the rail. There it stood, wings half-extended, a quizzical look in its eyes. Three feet was not a safe distance, but there was no time for a second attempt. The whistle screamed again. It sounded close enough for me to shake hands with the engineer. I ran down the center of the tracks, swiping at each bird as I passed.

Halfway to the most distant turkey, I received a double discouragement: the Flyer was too close for me to remain on the tracks any longer, and every bird I shooed from its path had returned to the rails.

If there was ever any doubt in my mind as to the total ignorance of turkeys, it was dispelled in the next minute. I slid down the track bed and crouched in the grass to watch the drama unfold. The turkeys were unconcerned as death approached. The only attention paid to the oncoming train was a chorus of gobbles in response to each blast from the Flyer's whistle. As the warnings grew more frequent and frantic, the turkeys gobbled longer and louder. Then, with the engineer sounding his whistle nonstop, with the ground shaking beneath me, train and turkeys came together.

I stared, amazed, as the foolish birds, like cheap displays of fireworks, exploded into pinwheels of white and red. Feathers coated the front of the Flyer as the death toll mounted. I could only hope none of the passengers were being served turkey for dinner.

The entire slaughter was shorter than most television commercials. Only one bird, the last one in line, tried to move. Some vague inkling of danger must have finally penetrated its miniscule brain, causing it to begin an awkward attempt at flight. The train caught it six feet off the ground, and then there were none. I climbed up the track bed to examine the carnage as the Flyer became part of the skyline. Massachusetts and Cricketts were doing the same.

"I never seen nothin' like it," marveled Massachusetts. "Them idjit birds just sat there an' got splattered."

"They wouldn't even make good stuffing now," lamented the boss.

"How we gonna clean up this mess?" asked Massachusetts.

My stomach quivered at the thought of the wretched burial ground.

"We ain't even gonna try," said Cricketts. "We're far enough away from the range so's not to bother the other birds. A few days from now there won't be nothin' left here but bones an' maggots."

Massachusetts chuckled. "When them maggots get good 'n fat, maybe we can find a reason to get bigmouth Books over here with a shovel."

"Yeah," Cricketts agreed, "that'd be good."

As we walked back to the range, where Spriggs was attempting a one-man roundup, I learned of Don Books's revulsion for maggots. Just the mention of them made him queasy. Cricketts told of Books finding a maggot-covered turkey wing in his lunch pail, and of certain unidentified individuals who liked to sprinkle maggots all over his motorcycle seat just before quitting time.

"I ain't much for practical jokin' around," Cricketts said, "but a puke like Books deserves whatever he gets."

I just hoped to still be around when they showed him the tracks.

The rest of my first day was routine, and I was thankful. What a way to get started on a job. During the first four hours I had witnessed murder, insanity, mass slaughter, and a sign from Heaven. How much could a guy stand? I would have given anything to be able to go back to the hotel, eat supper, and flop into bed. But that was not possible. The Chief had an announcement to make!

• • • •

A nervous anticipation filled the dining room as we sat around the table eating strawberry shortcake, waiting for the Chief. Speculation abounded as to where he was and what he might be doing. Belle said she was sure he must be in Sedalia finalizing his will. Dad wondered if maybe the Chief was seeing a doctor. The concern in their voices did not necessarily reflect what was in their hearts; I was sure they would regard any bad news as good news.

The aunts displayed a curious lack of interest in the guessing games. Was it possible they knew something we didn't? It seemed unlikely that Inez would keep information from Belle, but if the aunts had been ordered by the Chief to remain silent, they would obey. Of that I had no doubt.

Shortly after the hall clock struck the half-hour, we heard the front screen door squeak as it opened and closed. The dining room grew quiet, except for Fred clicking a spoon against his teeth hoping someone would notice his empty dessert dish.

The Chief looked almost regal as he marched through the doorway. The black suit he wore was a striking contrast to his white hair and mustache.

"Good, good," he said, assuming his position at the head of the table, "you're all here. I'm anxious to tell my news."

"Would you like strawberries, Poppa?" offered Julia.

"Nothing for me, thank you."

There was a short delay as he removed his suit coat and hung it over the back of the chair, along with his cane. He made a slight adjustment of a wall clock because it indicated he had arrived a minute late. All eyes were upon him. Belle's purple-lipped mouth hung open as she stared. She reminded me of a dog sitting in front of its dish, waiting to be fed. Dad chewed his lower lip. Mom sat stiff-backed, her face slightly flushed. The Chief took a sip of water and ended the torturous pause.

"When a man lives as long as I have, he often achieves a measure of success in some areas, but fails in others. The successes take care of themselves; the failures eat away at his insides. Many things I would change if I had it all to do over again, but there is one particular failure which causes me constant pain. Tonight I have taken a step which hopefully will be the beginning of correcting that failure."

He looked around the room, making eye contact with each of us, except Fred who was playing with a hole in his sock.

"Belle," he said suddenly, "what's the most precious gift a person can receive?"

The question caught her off-guard. I enjoyed watching her squirm.

"I . . . I . . . Well, money would be best, I suppose," she said.

The Chief turned to Dad. "What about you, Junior?"

"Me? Oh, let's see. Yeah, money would be hard to beat. I'd say money."

The old man laughed softly, in a manner suggesting he wasn't really amused.

"I don't agree with your answers," he said, "but I'm not surprised. They are part of the failure I mentioned a minute ago. This group, with certain exceptions, knows nothing of what is valuable in this world and what is not. Most of you would trade eternity for financial gain. Well, after Saturday night things might be different."

"What's Saturday night?" Dad asked, looking at the others rather than the Chief.

"I was coming to that. Saturday evening will kick off a time of new beginnings for this family as well as—"

"Oh boy," squealed Fred, "football!"

The Chief gave him a dismal stare. "Who said one word about football, young man?"

"You did. You said there was going to be a kickoff, so it has to be football. Who's your favorite team, Chief?"

My great-grandfather's jaw muscles bulged and quivered.

"Inez, give Fredric another helping of dessert."

"Yes, Poppa."

No sooner was the order given than it was carried out. Within seconds Fred was happily spooning strawberries and fluffy cake into the hole in his face. Another triumph for stupidity.

"Now as I was saying, on Saturday evening the Reverend Daniel Brady will be stopping in Climer as a last-minute extension of his Central Missouri Gospel Crusade. I've just now sewn up all the loose ends. There will be an old-fashioned gospel meeting which we will all attend. If my prayers are finally answered, there won't be any lost sheep in this flock come Sunday morning. Questions?"

Had the silence been any heavier, the floor would have collapsed. Belle appeared to be on the edge of cardiac arrest. My parents looked at each other in slack-jawed despair. Only the aunts seemed pleased. I found myself confused as to what, exactly, the Chief had said. Echoes of "crusade" and "lost sheep" reverberated across my gray matter. I was especially curious about that sheep business.

Julia gave the Chief a hug. "You're finally getting your wish, Poppa." Her eyes were shining.

"So far," he said.

The telephone rang in the kitchen. Belle seemed thankful for an excuse to leave the room.

"Poppa, have you been able to find out if Mrs. Brady will be coming along?" asked Inez.

"She won't be dining with us, but after she speaks at the Women's Auxiliary Dinner she will come to the hotel. You will all get to meet her."

Belle was back, pointing at the Chief. "Call for you."

Like a man forty years younger, the Chief strutted into the hallway. His cane still hung from the chair.

"I should have known," muttered Belle when he was out of sight. "That old fool will always have his own way, no matter what. He'll pump us full of religion or kill us trying. Well, to Hell with him."

Inez did a doubletake, and her mouth fell open.

"Wow!" said Fred.

"That's enough of that kind of talk in this house, little lady," snapped Julia in a voice I would never have thought her capable of producing.

Belle, blushing to a shade which nearly matched her lipstick, spun a half-circle and flounced out of the room. Her footsteps were heard all the way upstairs, as was the slamming of her bedroom door.

"I'm sorry you children had to hear that," apologized Julia in a more normal tone. "Sometimes Belle speaks without thinking. She shouldn't swear, and I'm afraid I lost my temper when I heard it."

"That's okay," Fred said. "Dad gets mad and cusses all the time. You should have heard him when his pants got all pink from—"

"I think we'll give Freddy an early bath tonight," interrupted Mom. "He's had a busy day, and it won't hurt him to get a little extra sleep."

"I hate extra sleep," protested Fred. Mom ignored his pleas, dragging him in the direction of the bathroom.

Normally I would have been overjoyed to see Fred dealt with in such a manner, but at that moment I felt only the onrushing effect of drowsiness. It came at me as fast as the Flyer had come at the turkeys. Like those birds, I made no attempt to move, allowing myself instead to be overtaken. It would have been interesting to hear further commentary concerning the great announcement, but my body was finished. All I remember is putting my head on the table to rest my eyes a minute. When I awoke, sunlight was streaming across our bed. It was 6:30 the following morning.

MISSOURI

*B*reakfast the next day was a somber affair. The Chief talked of nothing but the upcoming gospel meeting; the others stared at their plates, speaking only when necessary. No doubt the aunts would have shown some enthusiasm, but they were too busy running between the kitchen and dining room, as was their custom during meals.

My only thoughts were of old silver. Today something big was going to happen, I was certain of it. The assurance came from no less than the Big Man Himself. God, of course, not the Chief. While dressing for breakfast, I decided to ask Him if something would happen today concerning the old silver. I flipped my trusty quarter into the air, seeking heads as proof that some type of clue was forthcoming. The toss came up tails. It only took me a few seconds to realize that God wanted me to go two out of three. I got two heads in a row, and the issue was settled. What a wondrous Deity He was.

Halfway out the back porch door, on the way to work, I remembered my lunch. Julia had said there was a sack for me on the top shelf of the refrigerator. I looked inside the old Kelvinator and saw my lunch sitting beside a large green bowl of chicken and rice left over from last evening's meal. Like everything that Julia and Inez prepared, the food had been delicious, though now it looked less than appetizing. The chicken appeared rubbery, and the white rice was speckled with bits of congealed brown gravy. I stared at the bowl several seconds for no apparent reason; cold rice really isn't that fascinating a subject. Then my conscious half began to understand what my subconscious was trying to communicate.

After making sure no one was watching, I took a spoon from the silverware drawer and scooped a small amount of rice onto a piece of waxed paper. A rubber band helped hold the contents inside the wrapper. I dropped my little bundle into the lunch sack along with the spoon. After that, it was necessary to run all the way to the turkey farm to avoid being late.

• • • •

Cricketts had been right: nothing compared with working on a turkey farm. Whether it involved feeding turkeys, chasing them, or cleaning up after them, the work was unlike anything I had ever encountered. This morning we were given the opportunity to shovel slop from one of the empty sheds. Massachusetts, Spriggs, Don Books, and I waded in an ankle-deep swamp composed of bedding, manure, water trough overflow, and millions of feathers. Some of it was solid, some was liquid, and all of it was gaseous. As the four of us tossed the disgusting mess outside, Cricketts moved it with a loader tractor to a mountain of similar material occupying a far corner of the main yard. People would come in the Fall and pay good money for the privilege of filling buckets to sprinkle over lawns or gardens.

As one might suspect without ever having experienced it, shoveling slop was not a pleasant task. The very sight and smell of such work was enough to raise thoughts of seeking employment elsewhere. Standing in a pool of bubbly brown ooze that smelled worse than any place on earth—except the burial ground—pushed my nose and stomach to the brink of rebellion. But even if the sea surrounding us had possessed the color and fragrance of a strawberry milkshake, there would have been another burden to bear: flies were attracted to the shed like ants to spilled sugar. Buzzing, biting hoards of the bothersome insects infested our workplace, coating everything that wasn't in constant motion. As soon as body movement ceased, they landed on bare skin and sampled the flesh.

A lively breeze would have blown away most of our problems, but the morning air was humid and still. As temperatures inside the shed crept toward 100 degrees, flies and fumes were given maximum opportunity to drive us crazy. Tempers grew short.

"I don't know how they expect a man to do a job if he ain't got the right tools," complained Massachusetts. "The only way to get this heavier stuff outta here is to fork it. Cricketts is just too cheap to buy a couple forks, that's all. Just too dang cheap."

"Cry your guts out, you old fossil," said Don Books. "If you had a pitchfork you'd be yelling about getting a shovel. You're worthless."

"Know what, Booksie?" said Massachusetts, "if I had a mouth big as yours, I'd get me a job bein' a cave. You could charge little kids a dime to walk through it an' never have to work no more."

As usual, Don Books was no match for the barbed tongue of Massachusetts Conlon Rodgers. In much the same manner as an incensed Donald Duck, he erupted into a squawking, incoherent fit. He beat his shovel against the surface of the slop, and the air became filled with brown droplets.

"Knock it off, you crazy idjit," yelled Massachusetts as the malodorous spray rained upon him and Spriggs.

Books swung the shovel even harder and faster. Slop splattered my legs.

I had been preparing to empty my scoop when the commotion started. It was still suspended in midair. Like a knee reacting to a rubber hammer, I made an involuntary response and threw the contents into Books's face. For a second his head disappeared. Then his eyes blinked away their covering, and the whites stood out clearly against the brown. His mouth reappeared amid a spasm of choking and spitting.

"I'll kill you!" he screamed, although it took him several tries to get out all three words.

I knew he meant it. There was annihilation in his eyes that could not be mistaken for anything less. As he came toward me, I had little choice but to throw another load into his face and run for my life. Books screamed and made a blind dive in my direction. I jumped out the nearest door. Peripheral vision allowed me to see him surf across the mire on his chest. Once outside, I was tempted to stop and laugh. It was fortunate that I didn't because a dozen steps beyond the door I was stunned to look back and see my enemy stumbling out of the shed, dripping crud like some swamp monster and making sounds no normal person could ever have produced.

I ran as fast as fear could move me, but Books began gaining ground. His state of mind had evidently blown the lids off his adrenal glands. I could almost feel his livid breath scorching my neck as we rounded the far end of the shed. Only Cricketts saved me from a terrible whipping.

The boss was thirty feet down the road when I saw him. Luckily for me, his mood was not the best because the loader tractor had run out of gas. Seeing my predicament, Cricketts felt just ornery enough to let me pass before sticking his foot in front of the crazy man. Over my shoulder I saw Books turn a complete flip in the air and three somersaults on the ground. He came to rest against a wire fence. I turned around and came back to where the boss stood, hands on hips, looking down at Books. Massachusetts and Spriggs were there too.

"Get up on your feet, looneybird," ordered Cricketts.

On wobbly legs Don Books resumed a vertical position. He looked about as pitiful as was possible for a living human being. An outer layer of dry dirt coated an inner layer of slime. Except for the back of his legs, no part of him below the eyes was any color other than brown. Ugly brown. A passing stranger might have believed we just dug Books up from a premature grave.

"It was Books startin' the whole thing," Massachusetts told the boss. "He went nuts again, an' young Kane was just tryin' to cool him down."

Cricketts threw up his hands.

"I guess that just about tears it then, Books. I warned you five dozen times to quit goin' off the deep end, but you don't listen. I'm suspendin' you the next three days, an' after that we'll play it by ear."

Books pointed at me. "What about him?"

"Forget him. Massachusetts says you started it, so you pay."

"That lying old gummer is just protecting the punk because of Chief Kane, and so are you, Cricketts. You ain't nothing but one of the Chief's flunkies."

Cricketts's sunburned face darkened to the next shade of red.

I saw an opportunity to gain his favor while simultaneously implementing a plan of revenge. The scheme had been conceived earlier while I stared into Julia's refrigerator. It would begin with a bluff.

"As usual, you got everything all wrong," I said to Books. "Cricketts is a fair man, and he wouldn't do something unless it's right. He knows he doesn't need to protect me because I can take care of you anytime anywhere."

Books was incredulous.

"You saying you can whip me?"

"I'm saying I'm tougher than you are. I got more guts than you do."

"You're nuts," he sneered. "I may be crazy, but you're just plain nuts. Show me one way that you got more guts than me and I'll quit this place for good."

"Oh, man," said Massachusetts, "show him quick, before he changes his mind."

Things couldn't have worked out better if we had followed a script. Books's challenge opened a door which I intended to slam shut on his fingers. I told the group to stay put while I made a quick trip to the dungeon. In less than a minute I was back, a spoon protruding from my left hand. That unusual sight drew attention away from what was hidden inside my right fist.

"What's the deal with the spoon?" Books asked.

"Just follow me."

The four of them went with me to the far end of the shed we had been shoveling. In one corner was a disgusting maggot pile I had seen earlier. Thousands of squirming fly larvae were greedily feeding upon the rotting remains of a turkey.

"Looks like we missed one, boys," said Cricketts.

"That's one thing about maggots," Massachusetts said. "They don't ever miss a dead bird. They always find 'em."

Don Books stared at the wriggling, white mound in obvious discomfort. The stories of his revulsion for maggots had not been exaggerated.

"Show me how much guts you got now," I taunted him.

"Huh?"

"Pick up a handful of maggots and squish them between your fingers."

He looked at me the way I must have looked at him when he blew off the turkey's head. "I ain't touching those filthy things!"

"See there," I said to the others, "he's already chickened out. That proves I got more guts than him. Good-bye, Books."

Most of the fight had gone out of him, but he made one last attempt to salvage the situation.

"Hold the phone a minute, punk. You haven't got any more guts than me until you do it yourself. All you've done so far is shoot your mouth."

It was time to administer the *coup de grace*. I stepped to the edge of the maggot pile, brandishing the spoon.

"Any dud can squeeze maggots in his hands. But it takes real guts to do this."

Bending down to the pile, my back to the group, I made a quick scooping motion. The contents of my right hand were then discreetly deposited into the spoon. I held my breath throughout the maneuver because the smell in front of me was nauseating at close range.

"It doesn't count if you pick them up with a spoon," Books protested. "I could have done that."

I turned to him with the spoon in front of my face. The slightest trace of a smile touched his lips as he clung to the hope that I might be afraid to touch the maggots. The smile vanished in a splash of vomit when I stuck the spoon into my mouth, chewing the contents for all to see.

"What the . . ." mumbled Massachusetts. Cricketts could only jerk his head back and forth, as if that would make him see something other than what his eyes were showing him. Spriggs merely leaned against the wall, arms folded, like he saw guys eat maggots every day of his life. Some cool cat, that Spriggs.

When the last of the mouthful had been swallowed, I moved closer to Books. He had dropped to his knees and was looking up at me unbelieving, uncomprehending—like Fay Wray after her first glimpse of King Kong. He was a defeated man, groveling at the victor's feet.

"If you want me to, I'll finish off the whole pile," I said.

"No, no! I'm leaving anyhow . . . because of . . ."

Without bothering to finish his sentence, Don Books half-crawled, half-stumbled out the door. We watched in silence as he made his way toward the Harley-Davidson leaning against a dying elm between sheds 4 and 5. He barely had the strength to start it. Instead of sliding through the front gate and creating a dust cloud, as was his custom, he chugged out of sight without bothering to shift gears. I would never see him again.

"Kid," Massachusetts said after the motorcycle noise had faded, "you musta hated him awful bad to eat them maggots. That just ain't human."

"I don't think I'll ever get over seein' it," said Cricketts. "I just hope you got all of 'em chewed good, else they might tunnel their way back out."

I laughed at such an absurd thought, and pulled a small wad of waxed paper from my pocket.

"Just so you guys won't think I'm some kind of beast, I'll show you my secret." They watched without moving closer as I unwrapped the paper. "See . . . just white rice and gravy. That's all it was. I only pretended to be spooning up those maggots."

Massachusetts poked his finger at the rice to make sure it wasn't alive.

"Well, I'll be dogged," he said. "I'll be double-dogged an' fried in cracker crumbs."

He began laughing, as did Cricketts. Spriggs, still against the wall, put a hand to his mouth, coughed, whined, and laughed loudest of all. He snorted, howled, and stomped his boots.

"Rice," he said, wiping his eyes. "The dadgummed squirt was eatin' rice!"

Massachusetts slapped me on the back. "What a day this is, kid. We got rid of old Books, an' now Spriggsy is laughin' an' talkin' up a storm. This calls for a celerbration, don't it, Cricketts?"

"You betcha," agreed the boss. "You boys just go on over to the tower an' take it easy while I run to the house an' get us something to drink."

We left the shed in high spirits. I was a hero, and the glow of victory warmed my heart. As had been the case at the Battle of Little Mexico, I savored the sweet taste of revenge as long as possible. My surroundings had changed, my companions were different, but the joy of completing a successful mission was the same.

When Cricketts returned, I touched my bottle of Coke to their three Falstaffs and we toasted everything from white rice to Harry Truman's wife, Bess. It was a great time. Nearly three hours would pass before the elation of my triumph wore off and the inevitable post-revenge depression set in. Nearly four hours would pass before I realized Cricketts had inadvertently given me a gigantic clue as to where Lathom Kane's treasure was buried.

• • • •

I was halfway through the afternoon feeding chores, and pondering the fleeting quality of happiness. How come I didn't feel nearly so pleased with the defeat of Don Books as I had just hours ago? Where had the joy gone? It seemed to me that happiness was nothing more than a large, shimmering bubble afloat on the wind, reflecting bits of sunlight, enticing passersby into thinking it could be captured and caressed. But as soon as it was grasped, it would burst. A naive fool would be left with only a wet hand and a sense of having lost what was never truly possessed.

Belle or Dad would have understood. They had pursued a bubble of inheritance money as it appeared before them the past few days; it burst last night at the announcement of a gospel meeting. Weren't we all chasing some elusive bubble of happiness in one form or another? Grandpa had his booze, the Chief had his religion, and I had my acts of revenge. But none of them were permanent. Grandpa's early evening laughter always faded into melancholic mumblings. A God-trusting man like the Chief had spawned a family liberally sprinkled with heretics and blasphemers. My plans for revenge could only produce a few hours of satisfaction before confusion and unfulfillment invariably took control. Why was sweetness in the world so temporary, while bitterness lingered indefinitely? What chance did a guy have under such rotten conditions? The game of life was as rigged as the Wheel of Winners at the Hadleyville carnival; small wonder that people got drunk or went crazy or jumped off the local bridge. If only the happiness could be never-ending, the bubble eternal . . .

I was chin-deep in a rising river of self-pity before remembering one bubble that had yet to break. The dream of old silver—still alive and backed by the Man Upstairs—was tonic for a sagging spirit. I felt better, knowing this was one thing that couldn't go wrong. The Chief had told me in the little cemetery that God doesn't forget people. I knew He wouldn't forget my treasure either.

I checked my watch and saw there were twenty minutes remaining before a scheduled meeting with Cricketts. After our celebration ended, the boss had gone to Sedalia. He told us to meet him back in the tower at 3:30 to decide how to split up the work normally done by Don Books. I wondered if . . . TOWER!

The word suddenly jumped out at me like a monster in a 3-D movie. Twice Cricketts had used that word, and I nearly missed both clues. Lathom Kane's diary told of burying the old silver fifty paces off the back left corner of the tower. The ugly brick building with a collapsed rear wall and a snake-pit basement was my guidepost to riches. Who would ever have guessed?

I did a little yelling and jumping around, danced a victory jig, and kicked a few turkeys to express my elation. Then it occurred to me that such behavior might draw unwanted attention. A man with knowledge of buried treasure does not want to become part of a crowd. The smart thing to do would be to go find the back left corner of the tower and step off the fifty paces. When the exact location was discreetly marked, it would be simple enough to sneak back after-hours and dig up the loot. My heart pounded at the very thought.

As was usually my luck, a simple plan turned out to be complicated. Finding the left rear corner of the tower should have been the easiest part of the procedure, except that the back wall was no longer standing. Fallen bricks and twisted wood, lying in a dusty, vine-entangled pile, made it difficult to calculate precisely where the corner had been. I had to burrow down to the foundation to see where the cement blocks formed a right angle. My fingertips were gritty and raw by the time I finished. The meeting was going to start in ten minutes.

The next problem was to measure fifty paces. After determining the exact direction to be followed from the cornerstone, I began walking with slightly smaller steps than my normal stride. Julia had mentioned that Lathom Kane was a frail man and that he was in bad enough shape to enter a hospital. It seemed logical that his stride would be less than mine.

On the eleventh step, my toe brushed against the side of shed number 6. I stood there, my nose inches from the wall, wondering how to deal with this latest difficulty. A familiar voice spoke.

"Didn't ya see that shed sittin' there, kid?" asked Massachusetts.

"I seen it."

"Then how's come ya pert near bashed inta the side of it, an' how's come yer walkin' like somebody poured sand in yer underpants?"

"Uh, I'm pretending there's a firing squad, and they're marching me up against the wall to be shot. It's just a game."

Massachusetts rubbed the stubble on his chin and shot tobacco juice at a passing Monarch butterfly. "Yer really a pistol, kid, I'll say that much. Never know what yer gonna do next."

He walked away, talking to himself. I acted out the scenario of being blindfolded until he disappeared into the tower. Then it was back to business. I grabbed a twig off the ground and pushed it halfway through a tiny hole in the shed wall. This served as a marker, allowing me to run around to the other side of the wall, find the right spot, and continue my count. The same procedure was used on the opposite wall, and those of shed number 7.

By step thirty, I was becoming increasingly aware of a terrible smell. It was so strong, there was danger of losing the count. But I pinched my nostrils and concentrated harder on the ground beneath me. At step forty-three, the stench was so potent I smelled it through my mouth. The grass ended; I stepped down onto an irregular surface of brown dirt. At that point no amount of concentration could keep me from the realization that I was seven paces from the site of Lathom Kane's treasure—and the center of the turkey farm burial ground!

Belle would have been proud: my sense of greed was so intense that it kept me walking until the fifty paces were finished. Despite the loathsome atmosphere, I took the time to carefully mark the edge of the last step by pushing three pennies into the dirt. Then I turned and ran to the tower. I was two minutes late for Cricketts's meeting, and very close to throwing up.

The meeting wasn't any more than a realignment of jobs.

Cricketts decided that Spriggs would work exclusively with the range turkeys while I took care of the sheds. He and Massachusetts would hop back and forth between the two, helping out as needed. This was good news because it meant I would be on my own much of the time. Sneaking around after-hours to do my digging would not be necessary; it could be done on the job, if proper precautions were taken. Part of my task had been made easier, but nothing could change the location of the treasure. Digging was going to be a living nightmare.

On the way to the hotel late that afternoon, it came to me that God must be laughing His head off at my predicament. After getting rid of Don Books and discovering the location of the tower, I find out the riches are in the one spot I swore I'd never go. He promised I would find the old silver, but He didn't mention I would have to dig through a wretched, filthy graveyard to get it. Such irony probably gave God a few good guffaws, but all it gave me was an upset stomach and an uneasy feeling that persons entering into deals with Him had best read the fine print!

• • • •

About 7 that evening, Dad and I were heading for Grandpa's place to celebrate the old man's birthday. Fred wasn't feeling well, so Mom stayed at the hotel to care for him. That suited me fine; I had spent more than enough time with turkeys lately. It felt good to be alone with Dad. A week ago I would rather have eaten a pound of fishworms than be isolated with him. Now it didn't seem so bad. Since coming to Missouri, we hadn't been together as much, and seeing him humbled so often by his elders made him less intimidating somehow. Halfway to Sedalia I decided to test my newfound confidence by seeking answers to some nagging questions about the Kane family.

"Is Ruth my grandma?"

Dad gave me a blank stare. "Why would you think she's your grandmother?"

"She lives with Grandpa, don't she?"

"That stupid parrot Stan the Man lives with him too, but that don't mean he's your grandmother."

His voice was harsh and cold. I felt all the old anxieties growling inside my gut once more. The smart thing might have been to drop the issue, but I was determined to push ahead with the questioning. If it cost me a slap in the mouth, so be it. After what Don Books had wanted to do to me earlier in the day, getting slapped seemed a small enough consequence.

"If she's not my grandma, who is she?"

Dad lit a cigarette.

"Ruth Silversprings is a woman who walked into your grandfather's place about six years ago and never left. They just live together and don't care what anybody thinks about it. He says he loves her, and when he dies she'll get the gas station and anything else that's left. I say she's just a gold digger who's waiting for the payoff."

"Is that the same as everybody waiting for the Chief to die?"

Smoke must have went down the wrong pipe because Dad coughed and turned red in the face.

"It's different when it's blood relation," was all he said.

"Where's my real grandma then?"

"Dead. She died when I was in the army. When I came back for the funeral, Grandpa was drunk. We got into a heckuva fight. I didn't speak to him for almost three years, and by then I was married and living in McKinley. That was a long time ago."

He flicked his cigarette out the window.

"Is that why the Chief hates Grandpa, because he's just a drunk?"

Dad hit the brakes, sliding the Buick onto the shoulder of the road amid a swirl of dust. A car behind us swerved, honking its horn. Dad grabbed the front of my shirt and jerked me toward him.

"If you ever call him a drunk again, I'll beat you to a pulp. You got that?"

"Yes, sir!"

I didn't use a formal answer to be cute, but because I was truly sorry for having said the wrong thing. That must have been clear; Dad released my shirt. The ride resumed in silence.

"Did I tear anything?" he finally asked.

"No."

"Good. I didn't mean to get so mad, Tom, but I've heard him

insulted too many times by too many people who've never had to walk in his shoes."

"Like Belle? She calls him an outcast."

"Belle's got a big mouth. She isn't exactly the most popular person on the face of the earth. Grandpa's worth ten of her kind. He's just had a cloud hanging over his head that won't ever go away."

"What happened?"

"He killed his brother."

Dad said it as calmly as if he were talking about killing weeds in a garden. I studied his face to be sure he wasn't attempting some sick joke.

"How?" I asked him.

"Well, it wasn't anything but an accident. When he was about thirteen, your grandfather took a wagon and a team of horses to a little town called Archer to pick up some furniture the Chief had bought for the hotel. Your great-grandmother, Eleanor Kane, rode along, and so did Paul, the youngest son."

At the mention of Paul, I remembered the weathered tombstone marked "Paul Jamison Kane." I also remembered the Chief's tears.

"On the way home from Archer there was an accident. The wagon missed a curve and overturned. Paul Kane was crushed to death. Grandpa and his mother were thrown clear and didn't get hurt. But Eleanor went into shock when she saw what had happened to her son. They kept her in bed for weeks after that. Julia once told me that any mention of Paul sent Eleanor into hysterics, even years later. After the funeral, the Chief made it clear he would never forgive Grandpa for the rest of his life. That's the way it's been ever since."

"How come Grandpa stayed around here all these years then?"

"I asked him that once. He said he still loved the Chief, and just hoped that someday things would get worked out."

Dad's voice cracked. It was obvious how deeply he felt the plight of Grandpa Kane. I couldn't imagine loving someone who hated me, not for all those years anyway. It certainly helped me understand why Grandpa was so sad all the time, and I knew I must forgive him completely for what had happened at the carnival. The last thing he needed was more guilt thrown onto the pile.

When we pulled into the decrepit gas station, Grandpa was standing in the doorway turning over an OPEN sign so it read CLOSED. He waved as we got out of the car.

"Where's Louise an' the boogernose?"

"One's sick and one's playing nurse," Dad said.

"Sounds like me an' old Ruthie," joked Grandpa. Nobody laughed.

The old man looked at me with an expression that said he wasn't quite sure where he stood after what happened the last time we were together. I did an uncharacteristic thing to make my feelings clear: I walked over to him and administered a tight hug.

"Happy birthday, Grandpa."

We held on to each other longer than a couple in a marathon dance. Squeezing his tired bones, I realized how much I loved this forlorn little man. Dad nodded his approval at what I had done, appreciative of how I handled the situation.

Grandpa finally released me. "Hey, let's quit standin' around an' get at that cake Ruthie's got in there. It's chocolate, with ten hundred candles growed out the top."

We went inside where Ruth stood behind the bar smiling, just like the other time we were there. She wore the same checkered dress. Her presence seemed ornamental, as if Grandpa kept her in a closet and only put her on display when company came. I said hello, and she returned the greeting; there was no exchange between her and Dad.

"We got us a place all fixed up," Grandpa said, pointing to a corner booth with several streamers of crepe hanging down each side. A candle-covered cake in a rectangular pan sat on the table, along with three plates and three forks. "What'll ya have to drink, Junior?"

"Schlitz is fine."

"How 'bout you, Tommy?"

"Got any more Dr. Pepper?"

"Does a dog got fleas? Course we got Pepper. Ruthie, bring a Schlitz, a Pepper, and a Squirt for me." We must have looked shocked because he laughed and explained, "I'm on the wagon tonight. Figure if my family is gonna put up with me on my birthday, then I should at least stay sober an' help 'em suffer through it."

Ruth brought the drinks, along with glasses of ice. As we poured, she returned to the bar.

"To a happy sixty-seventh year," Dad toasted.

"To a *complete* sixty-seventh year," corrected Grandpa. "When you look like I do, you just try to make it all the way to the end, happy or not." He took a gulp of pop and grimaced. "Man oh man, I'm glad I usually drink liquor instead of sodee. This stuff could ruin a guy."

After our toast, we ate huge slabs of cake which Grandpa cut for us. Dad said the pieces were too big, but Grandpa said a chunk of cake could never be too big. I liked his way of thinking.

Eventually the conversation turned to events of the previous evening at the hotel. Dad started to tell about the Chief's announcement, but Grandpa knew all about it.

"Julia gave me a call afterwards," he explained. "I bet ol' Belle was havin' kittens when she found out Poppa wanted to save her soul an' not her pocketbook."

"You got that right," I said. "She cussed Julia and got kicked out of the room."

Grandpa chuckled, "I bet she'll be fun to live with the next few days."

"Well," Dad said, "I have to admit, the whole business kind of got to me too. I wouldn't have ever guessed that we were going to hear about religion."

"It couldn't have been nothin' else, Junior. When Poppa gets somethin' in his head, he'll keep it there till he dies. I know that for a fact. He's the original Missouri mule."

Dad drained the rest of his beer and belched. "Of all the things a man could be fanatical about, why did he have to choose religion? I'd rather live in a cardboard box and eat potato peelings than be one of those church phonies who thinks a good time is singing hymns or saying a prayer every thirty seconds. What kind of stuff is that for a normal human being to do? If there really was a God, He'd get so bored with them all that He'd probably make a Hell just to get rid of everybody."

Without having to be asked, Ruth brought Dad another Schlitz. Grandpa eyed it longingly while taking a halfhearted sip from his own drink. Dad must have been thinking hard on the religious issue because he gave an absentminded "thanks" to Ruth as she served him.

"There is a God, Junior," Grandpa said after a while.

My head turned around so fast that my neck popped. Dad couldn't have looked any more shocked had Grandpa admitted to being Batman. "Are you sure that drink isn't spiked?" he said.

"Wish it was, Junior, 'cause it's harder to talk serious when I'm sober. Fact is, I was half-boomed up 'bout a year back when I started thinkin' maybe there was a God. I figured it was just the booze talkin', but when I got straightened out the next day, it still made some sense to me. That's where I'm at right now."

"What changed your mind?" Dad asked.

"Stars an' marigolds."

His answer struck me funny, and I laughed. So did he. Dad remained serious. "I don't get what you mean by that," he said.

"Well, it's this way . . . I was plantin' marigold seeds one day, an' it came to me that them seeds were amazin' things. They don't look like much, but after they're growed they make some of the purtyest flowers you ever seen. I started wonderin' what makes a seed work. Don't exactly know why I started wonderin' . . . I been plantin' 'em since I was a kid an' I never wondered before.

"Then a few nights later I was drinkin' again, an' I decided to go outside an' sit in the grass. There was a good enough breeze to keep the bugs off, so I just laid back an' happened to look up at the stars. It was a clear sky, an' there was four jillion stars shinin' if there was one. I seen the Big Dipper, the little one, an' for a while I thought I saw a 1928 Packard, but I wouldn't swear to it in a court of law. Anyhow, I started gettin' this question in my head about who made them stars. I may just be an old drunk, but them stars hadta get up there somehow, an' I know people didn't do it. I decided right then that somewhere in the sky is a big Potentate who runs things down here. I ain't sayin' I like how He's runnin' it, but I know He's there."

By the time he finished the explanation, Grandpa was sweating heavily, as if such an admission was hard labor. He drained the Squirt and asked Ruth for a Coke with ice.

"Do ya think I'm nuts, Junior?" he said as Ruth handed him his drink.

"No. I guess I'm just surprised that you're talking so different from what you always told me before."

"Yeah . . . well, maybe I'm just gettin' smarter with age. I put lotsa seeds in the dirt, an' I seen stars every night of my life, but it took sixty-some years to figure out there was somethin' special about 'em."

I began squirming as the urge to reveal my own dealings with God became quite strong. I didn't want to say too much, for obvious reasons, but it was impossible to keep completely quiet.

"I believe in God too."

"Well, well," Grandpa said in an exaggerated manner that sounded like an attempt to imitate Groucho Marx, "the plot thickens. Might as well jump in the soup with the rest of us meatballs, Junior."

Dad shrugged. "Maybe there is a God, but so what? I don't see Him doing anybody any good. People kill each other every day, families don't get along, so why do we need Him? I say let's take another vote and get somebody up there who'll do the job right."

"I'll drink to that," Grandpa said.

I lost all track of time as we discussed further the issues of God and religion. Ruth must have gotten her fill of homespun theology; she went behind the yellow blanket and turned on the television. Grandpa became nervous and fidgety as the evening passed. His hands grew shaky. His carefree frame of mind slowly evaporated, and he appeared distracted. Dad noticed it too.

"Better have a drink," he told his father softly.

The old man looked at us with the sad expression we knew so well.

"I wanted to do good for ol' Tommy here. Guess I ain't as tough as I thought."

"You did good, Grandpa," I said, "but now you should drink something. It's all right . . . I don't mind."

I never thought I would hear myself encouraging someone to drink, but I had never before seen a man suffering the shakes. Especially a loved one, enduring it on my account.

Grandpa hesitated another minute, then got up and fixed himself a drink at the bar. He downed it in a hurry and made a second. The shakiness was less noticeable as he returned to the booth.

"Ya know what the craziest thing is about this whole God business, Junior?" he said.

"What's that?"

"The fact that I didn't figure it out when it could have done me some good. When I was younger, I mighta had a shot at Heaven, if it's really there. I coulda lived a decent life, maybe gone to church a few times, an' been good enough to sneak through the Pearly Gates. But no, I wait till I got sins piled halfway to the moon before I start believin' in God. Is that stupid or what?"

"Maybe you still got time," I said. "If you don't sin anymore from now on, and you live as long as the Chief, there might be a chance you could come out ahead."

Grandpa waved his hand, indicating the situation was hopeless.

"Heaven should only be for the good guys, Tommy, an' Hell should be for the rest of us. A kid like you still has a chance to do all right an' get a place earned up there. But me an' your dad are Hell-bound for sure."

Dad looked up from his drink. "Let's don't be in such a hurry to make reservations. I might still have a chance, you know."

It was then that Ruth stuck her head out from behind the yellow blanket and told Grandpa the wrestling matches were on television.

"Cryin' out loud," he said, jumping up and knocking over a couple of empty beer bottles, "I forgot all about 'em. We gotta see these, Junior . . . It's Bozo Henry against Killer Kremlin, plus a buncha other good ones."

Dad wasn't much of a professional wrestling fan, but he humored Grandpa. We spent an hour watching men maul each other. When the wrestling was over, so was our evening. Grandpa escorted us to the car in a whiskey-warmed glow.

"This was the best night I had in years," he kept saying.

We hugged him, shook his hand, and still he didn't want to let us go. Dad practically had to shut the Buick's door on his fingers to finally get away.

"Grandpa must really miss us when we leave," I said as we drove down the blacktop toward Climer.

"He just worries that he might not ever see us again, that's all."

"Why would he think that?"

"Because he's dying."

For the second time in one night, Dad had shocked me with a cold-blooded statement linking Grandpa with death.

"Dying from what?"

"Booze. Two doctors have already told him that his organs are so bad he could drop dead anytime. Especially if he keeps drinking."

The bad news almost made me sick to my stomach. I remembered having told Grandpa earlier to go ahead and take a drink.

"Then how come he doesn't stop?"

"Why should he bother?" Dad said.

"So he won't die . . . So he can live!"

Dad looked at me in the dimness of the dashboard lights. "I don't think Grandpa is sure if he wants to live or not. Life has given him a lot of cheap shots over the years, and people he loves have hurt him more than you could ever imagine. We've all let him down."

"Even you?"

"Especially me. With his own father hating him so much, he needed a son who would love him. But I'm afraid I was like everyone else. I blamed him for all the things that weren't right with my own life. When my mother died of cancer, I had it in my mind that Grandpa was the cause. He needed me then, but we had that fight I told you about, and I ended up walking out on him. I didn't come back until the Chief wrote to tell me Eleanor Kane was dying. You were just a few months old then. We stayed at the hotel and helped out as best we could until Eleanor died. Those were ugly days. Grandpa wanted to be near his mother, but the Chief kept him away from everything. It's a wonder he didn't crack."

"Did you make up with Grandpa then?"

"Partly. It hurt me to see him being treated so bad, but that was another reason why I was always mad at him. I never understood how he could stand to take so much abuse from the Chief."

"Sometimes it ain't easy to tell your dad to lay off," I said.

He looked surprised, as if it had never occurred to him that I might have reason to consider such a thing.

"Do you remember the first day we came to the hotel, when we took the luggage upstairs to the bedrooms?" he asked.

"Yeah."

"Do you remember your mother telling you how we almost bought a house in Climer?"

"I remember getting shoved away when I tried asking a question about it."

Dad cleared his throat and pulled at his collar.

"Well, I guess I should have explained myself, but there was so much you didn't know then. I didn't feel like going through the whole business about Grandpa and the Chief, but you know most of it now."

"Except why you left Climer that last time."

The breeze was getting cool, so I rolled up my window. We rode in silence until he was ready to finish the story.

"The day of Eleanor Kane's funeral," he said at last, "I stood with Grandpa, trying to give him strength. It was hot, and the wind was blowing very hard. Dust coming off the dirt pile by the grave was getting into people's eyes. Everyone looked like they were just trying to make it through the services . . . except the Chief. He sat there staring at the coffin, like he was alone in his room. After the preaching was finished, people came over to him to offer their sorrows and sweet talk, but he acted like it was just him and that coffin. Finally there wasn't anybody left but him and Grandpa and me. I told Grandpa we better go, but he said he had something to tell the Chief first. He said it in a strange way, a way I didn't understand. I watched him go to his father and say something that didn't take any more than fifteen seconds."

Dad stopped talking to wipe his eyes with his fingers. I should have waited until he was ready to continue, but the suspense was more than my heart needed to bear.

"So what happened?"

"I can still see it," he whispered hoarsely. "The Chief took his cane and hit Grandpa right across the face. He knocked him down and kept hitting him until I ran over and took the cane away. He looked like a crazy man, and Grandpa looked like he got hit by a truck. I think that was the worst moment of my life."

"But why did the Chief hit him?"

"I never knew. Neither one would talk about it. Julia and Inez were still married back then, but they practically lived at the hotel the next couple weeks trying to get the Chief to bring everything out in the open. But he refused. I was so sick of the whole stupid feud that I told your mother we were going back to McKinley. It's bad enough that people want to live like that, without their families watching it and having to wipe up the blood each time. But that's what happened, and that's the way things are today. You can see why Grandpa might not be too worried about living longer. All things considered, what does he really have to live for?"

That question kept me awake much of the night. Who could answer such a thing?

MISSOURI

*T*he day I had been waiting for, fantasizing about, dreaming of was also a day to be dreaded. Glittering thoughts of buried treasure were dulled by the specter of an abominable graveyard. Throughout the morning feeding chores I maintained the appearance of business as usual while mentally preparing to dig for old silver. A dozen dead turkeys, in various states of decay, had been discovered during a careful search of the sheds. Stuffing them into a burlap sack was a disgusting job, but they would serve to camouflage my real reason for entering the burial grounds.

Just before 12, as the others walked toward the tower to eat, I asked Cricketts if it would be possible to work through lunch and get off an hour earlier. He agreed. Five minutes later I was stuffing cotton balls up my nose and wrapping a handkerchief around my head to help cover my mouth. A pair of gloves would protect my hands from whatever might have to be touched during the digging. My plan was to locate the treasure and move it to one of the empty sheds near the main gate. Leaving work early would then allow me to haul my precious cargo away undetected. I dared to hope that things might proceed smoothly, but problems arose immediately.

The cotton balls and handkerchief had a minimal effect against the horrid stink surrounding me. The smell was so penetrating that it bothered my head even more than my stomach. Each time I leaned over the shovel, my skull felt as if it was parting down the middle. Conditions were aggravated by the slowness of the digging. As the spade bit into the dirt, its full thrust was often blunted by the striking of a bone or beak or claw from some previously interred bird. Separated body parts were fairly easy to remove from the path of descent; those that were still connected to a turkey had to be grasped with both hands and uprooted. The result was a stiff grotesque corpse whose ratty plumage was infested by a variety of scavenging insects.

The sun was also a hindrance. Directly above, it seemed intent on melting me over the brown dirt like butter over a baked potato. I sweated so much that the handkerchief kept sliding down to my chin. The hotter I got, the deeper I breathed and the more affected I became by death fumes seeping out of the ground. The smart thing would have been to take frequent breaks, but there was no time for that. I needed to be finished before the lunch hour ended.

At ten minutes to 1 I was shoulder-deep into the ground, and exhausted. My muscles were quivering, and my hands had blistered inside the gloves. I was no longer aware of the smell around me. Nor was I aware of Massachusetts Conlon Rodgers, until he spoke.

"You buryin' turkeys or diggin' a canal?"

"Burying." My throat was dry, and talking was not pleasant.

"You could drop a car in that hole an' still have room for ever' dead bird on the place. Get up outta there an' take a blow."

I was too weak to climb, so Massachusetts had to pull me out by the arms. We walked to the closest upwind tree and sat in the shade. I unwrapped a piece of Blackjack Gum to kill the taste in my head. He began a systematic spraying of brown juice upon a patch of fluffy gray dandelions.

"I thought we was friends," he said after a dozen spits.

"We are."

"Not likely. Friends don't hold out on each other."

"What's that supposed to mean?"

"It means I ain't a idjit like Booksie was. I wondered right off the bat why a kid like you was workin' here, but ya gave me a sob story 'bout a carnival, so I figgered I'd wait an' see. I keep on noticin' how yer always snoopin' 'round, like somethin' got lost, an' then yesterday I seen ya walkin' weird, like ya was measurin' off steps. Now I catch ya diggin' a hole that's fifty times bigger 'n it oughta be. It don't add up, kid."

I avoided his eyes, trying to think, but he had me. Even if I didn't confess, he would watch me so closely in the future that completing my plan would be impossible. I didn't have the strength or the desire to pretend any longer, so I let him in on my precious secret.

"I've been looking for buried treasure."

He spit so hard that the whole wad came out of his mouth. Dandelion fuzz flew everywhere. "Treasure? Is that what I heard?"

"Yeah."

"What kind of treasure?"

"Silver."

"Yer pullin' my leg, ain't ya, kid?"

"Look, it's bad enough I gotta tell this without having to talk you into believing me."

Massachusetts stared at me a while, then got to his feet.

"I'm startin' to get this jingle in my hip, like I do playin' poker when I know I'm gonna fill a straight or a flush. I believe ya, kid. But how do ya know there's silver 'round this place?"

I told him about Lathom Kane's diary. He paced, grunting periodically. When the explanation was finished, he loaded another wad into his cheek and sat back down.

"Somethin' ain't kosher 'bout all this."

"Why do you say that?"

"Ain't no treasure buried in this stinkin' place. Ain't possible."

I was getting irritated. Not only had my secret been revealed, but now its authenticity was being disputed. The only thing worse than having an accomplice was having a know-it-all accomplice.

"I counted fifty paces exactly," I said. "It has to be here. I just need to go a little deeper."

"That's what I mean, kid. It won't do no good to go deeper or left or right or anyplace. I was here five years ago when they first dug this hole out to make a graveyard. Cricketts had a guy come in here with one of them diggin' machines. They dug up most of this field an' musta went down ten feet. The idea was to throw the dead ones in an' cover 'em up as we went along. I know they didn't find no treasure when they first dug this place, else Cricketts 'd be in Tijuana by now. An' it don't figure that yer uncle'd have buried the stash any further down than that. It just don't add up."

"All I know is, the diary said fifty paces off the left rear corner of the tower. Buildings only have one left rear corner, don't they?"

"Maybe, maybe not," Massachusetts said, in the manner of one who knows more than he's telling. "Let's go take a look."

I didn't know what another look at the tower could accomplish, but there was little else to do. If Massachusetts had seen the entire burial ground excavated to ten feet, further digging would be pointless. Thoughts flickered that the diary was a hoax and the signs from God were merely the results of wishful imagination. But faith persisted, especially after what we were soon to discover.

Massachusetts walked slowly along one side of the tower, then checked the opposite wall. He carefully examined the bricks in the area closest to the collapsed section.

"Here's the trouble." He pointed to a place where the bricks were slightly different in color and texture from those closer to the front. "These here bricks are newer that them other kind, an' they match the ones layin' on the ground. I seem to remember Cricketts sayin' somethin' 'bout his brother-in-law doin' some brickwork years back, an' one night durin' a storm the whole thing caved in. I don't know that he was talkin' 'bout the tower, but there ain't no other place on the farm that gots bricks."

It made sense. The bricks on the ground had been erected and fallen long after Lathom Kane died. The corner he had measured from eventually became part of a longer wall, most of which was now collapsed. The difference in starting places would alter the final destination. Perhaps the new location would be outside the perimeter of the graveyard.

"Massachusetts, you're fabulous."

"It's been said before, kid, but mostly by the ladies."

I slapped his back, promising a share of the silver for his brilliant deduction. No mention was made as to what exactly comprised a share, but it was understood that he would soon be able to buy a finer brand of chaw. We shook hands and prepared for the second step-off.

It was necessary to knock out a few loose bricks to find the exact edge of the old corner. My new partner handled that while I stood watch in case Cricketts or Spriggs came along. When the space was properly cleared, I leaned my back against the points of the bricks and began another count to fifty. The same problems arose with the sheds blocking our path, but an extra pair of legs made the solution much simpler.

Starting in a different spot did, indeed, eliminate the need for further entries into the burial ground. I reached fifty paces just beyond a barbed-wire fence that separated National Poultry Incorporated from a neighboring farm. The hole I had been digging minutes before lay, like an open sore, twenty feet to my left. The air was still polluted, but there would be no bodies to dig through. I felt anticipation building. Massachusetts didn't seem to notice.

"We should wait till tomorrow . . . Do it the smart way."

"Wait for what?"

"Well, I got me this tool over to home. It's shaped like a long T, an' it's used fer findin' underground water tiles. I figger we could be a few feet off-line one way or t' other, an' we'd save us a ton of diggin' if we let that thing do the findin'."

"Yeah, but I don't want to wait. It's right here under my feet, I just know it is."

He shrugged, leaning back against a wooden post in the fence. "More power to ya."

I took the spade and started throwing dirt like a backhoe. Compared to previous attempts, this was shamefully simple. In a matter of minutes I was down two feet.

"If she's there, I wouldn't expect ya'd have to go much farther," Massachusetts said.

"She's there. Don't worry."

When the spade hit something solid, Massachusetts came off the fencepost in a hurry. I shoveled even faster; my heart threatened to suck my veins flat.

We could see that the top of the object was metallic and rounded.

"See if ya can pull her up," urged my partner.

I tossed the spade aside and shoved my fingers underneath the edge. One jerk was all it took to unearth an old hubcap.

"Some treasure," scoffed Massachusetts.

I ignored him and resumed digging. Somewhere near four feet deep it became clear this was not the spot. I pounded my fist against the side of the hole. Massachusetts cleaned his fingernails with a pocketknife, waiting for me to admit the wisdom of his suggestion.

"All right, so we'll do it tomorrow," I said, climbing back to ground level.

"Just as well. I play poker on Friday nights, an' if I had me a treasure I'd probably lose it all to a full house. This way I'll get to keep it a whole week."

"Yeah, well don't forget to bring that T thing to work in the morning."

"I won't. Hey, ya think maybe that T stands fer treasure?"

"Might. Let's hope so."

I would have checked with God right then, to be sure, but my lucky quarter was lying on the dresser in bedroom number 6.

• • • •

Julia and Inez cooked spaghetti for supper. After two helpings, I had to let my belt out a notch. Another week at the hotel and I would be shaped like Hippo Reeves.

The Chief, as he had since the great announcement, dominated mealtime conversation with talk of the gospel meeting. For the umpteenth time he reminded us of exactly when the preacher was expected to arrive tomorrow. Instruction was given the aunts as to what foods should be prepared and how the seating was to be arranged. Fred and I were given special tutoring on how to address the preacher. We were to call him "Reverend Brady"; nothing else would be acceptable.

"I suppose Mr. Kennedy has the same problem when the Queen of England visits," mocked Belle. "Now let me see . . . Do we call her 'Your Highness' or 'Your Majesty' or just plain 'Queenie'?"

The Chief pointed a forkful of spaghetti her way.

"You may refer to the Queen in whatever manner you wish, but the Reverend Brady will be called 'Reverend Brady.' Also, Belle, try to resist the temptation of filling the bathroom with your cigarette smoke while our company is here. I don't want him thinking an old fire chief's house is on fire."

His remark made Fred laugh and Belle blush. Mom remained expressionless, but I knew she was smiling inside. She mentioned once that Belle thought the Chief wasn't aware of her clandestine smoking binges behind the bathroom door. How foolish to underestimate the old boy after living with him so long. Anything he didn't know about the hotel wasn't worth knowing in the first place.

While Inez distributed bowls of warm cherry cobbler, I decided to risk causing some trouble. As one just hours away from being independently wealthy—and therefore unconcerned about getting on the Chief's good side—it fell upon me to ask an awkward question.

"Has anyone invited Grandpa to the gospel meeting?"

There was a silent pause as everyone momentarily froze in the middle of what they were doing; teeth stopped chewing, arms became suspended across the table, and conversation died. It was like watching a home movie and having the film stick. Then the action suddenly resumed, but things were too precise and proper.

"The plans have already been made, Thomas Jamison," said the Chief. "They do not include him."

"I thought this was supposed to be for the whole family."

The film stuck again, and it remained stuck as everyone at the table realized a confrontation was imminent. The Chief methodically laid down his fork, touched a napkin to his lips, and tried to stare me down.

"Are you presuming, young man, to tell me how to run the affairs of my own family?"

"I just don't know why Grandpa can't come, that's all."

He pounded the table with his fist. "What you don't know would fill the shelves of every library on the North American continent. I make the decisions around here, and I make them so people like you will see the light and hopefully move toward it. The choices I make may not be the most popular ones, but they are the correct ones. Your grandfather has no business at the gospel meeting. His presence would only serve to undermine what we're trying to accomplish. You, of all people, should know how capable he is of encouraging someone to play the fool."

Like Belle before me, I blushed at the Chief's caustic comments. Unlike Belle, I did not have to curb my tongue to protect future financial gains.

"Maybe we should ask Reverend Brady what he thinks about keeping Grandpa out."

Mom actually gasped when I said that, as if she couldn't believe her oldest child would say such a thing to God Almighty, Jr. Dad ordered me to the bedroom, but there was a strange lack of anger in his voice. The Chief tried getting in the last word as I left the table.

"If we allow a spoiled apple to mix with the good fruit, it will soon contaminate the ones around it."

"I'll remember that the next time I bake an apple pie." I was already in trouble—I might as well go out with a bang.

Someone must have started after me because the Chief gave the command to "let him go." It could have been Mom or Dad, but it also could have been Julia, who fifteen minutes later knocked on my bedroom door.

"I hope you're not too upset," she said, sitting on the side of the bed.

"I'm fine, Julia."

"Good. Now, I shouldn't be up here because Poppa wouldn't like it. But I wanted to say that you were right about Johnny coming to the services tomorrow night. He should be allowed to participate. I'm driving into Sedalia later to visit a friend in the hospital. On my way back I will stop at your grandfather's and invite him to come hear Reverend Brady."

"What will the Chief say?"

"I don't believe he'll even have to know." She winked at me from behind her glasses, squeezing my forearm. "Thank you for caring enough about Johnny to stand up to Poppa. That isn't an easy thing to do."

When she left I laid down on the bed, marveling at how much was still to be learned about my relatives. Who would have thought Julia capable of plotting a deception of the Chief, no matter how worthy the cause? That was almost as strange as hearing Grandpa referred to as "Johnny." The name didn't seem to fit him. I closed my eyes and tried to think of a first name that would sound good on him. My brain smoked, but nothing came. Nothing at all, except two hours of dreamless sleep.

• • • •

The sun, just touching the western horizon, shone through the window, turning the inside of my eyelids orange. I was never sure if that was what woke me or if it was the sound of a car sliding across the graveled drive below. I looked outside and saw Julia was back. She had left long skid marks that stretched to the street. Julia was normally a very cautious driver.

As I turned away from the window, she slammed the car door. It sounded like a rifle shot. Something wasn't right. I ran downstairs, reaching the kitchen just as she stomped through the back door.

"Hello, Julia."

She walked past me like I died last week. The funny little hat she wore—white with artificial flowers pinned to it—sat halfway back on her head like a bus driver's.

"Where is your great-grandfather?" she called over her shoulder.

"I don't know, I just came—"

"POPPA!" She blasted out the word like a Marine drill instructor.

It seemed I should still be in bed sleeping because this couldn't be real. If I didn't know better, it would have been within the realm of possibility to guess that Julia had sipped a few suds. Inez came trotting down the hall, wide-eyed and confused.

"Sister, what is the matter?"

"I want Poppa!"

"Well, dear, I'm not sure where he's at. Belle and Junior took Freddy over to the store for—"

"POPPA!"

Julia left us behind, marching down the hallway toward the lobby. The Chief met her at the stairs.

"I'm not deaf yet, Julia," he scolded. "There is no need to—"

"I've just come back from Johnny's, and he told me something that I could hardly believe. I want you to verify it for me if you can."

The only sound to be heard was the tapping of Julia's foot. The Chief watched it as if mesmerized by its motion.

"Say your piece," he said softly.

"I certainly will." She took a deep breath. "After my hospital visit, I stopped at Johnny's and asked him to attend the gospel meeting. He said nobody would want him there, but I assured him we would *all* want him there because he is one of us. I told him to forget about what he did all those years ago and to start thinking of the future. And do you know what he said to me then?"

"What?" Inez and I asked simultaneously. The Chief said nothing.

"Johnny said he didn't have anything to forget because he never did anything wrong to begin with."

"He's a drunken, shameless liar!" snarled the Chief, a blue vein visibly throbbing at his temple.

"He said," continued Julia, "that he was not the one driving the wagon when Paul was killed."

"But, sister," said Inez, "nobody else was there but Momma." She stared blankly at Julia. Then her jaw dropped. "He can't mean that Momma was responsible?"

Julia nodded vigorously. "Our mother was driving the wagon that took one brother's life and ruined another's."

Without warning the Chief's hand smacked against Julia's cheek, leaving a white imprint upon her pink flesh. My aunt stood her ground, determined, almost defiant. I was totally shocked. A fifty-four-year old fact was being called a lie, and the Chief had slapped his beloved eldest daughter. What next?

"Can't you see what he's doing?" croaked the old man. "He's trying to win sympathy and turn you against me by creating this monstrous lie about his own mother."

"That isn't true, Poppa. Johnny knows me well enough to understand that nothing could ever have turned me against you, except your own cruelty. I loved you as much as any human being on earth, my dear husband included, and that love kept me from speaking out all these years since the accident. I used to cry about the way you treated our brother, but I was afraid to talk about it. Besides, I always believed him to be guilty of a reckless, deadly act. Now I know the truth, Poppa."

Inez anxiously waved a hand in front of her sister's face. Julia stopped talking to let her speak.

"I'm as shocked as you are, sister, and it's going to be a long time before this settles in my mind. But I don't see how Poppa can be held responsible. He must be just as surprised as the rest of us."

"If only he was," said Julia. "But the fact is, Poppa has known about this for thirteen years. He has known since the day Momma was buried."

"Is that true, Poppa?" demanded Inez.

The Chief answered, but with far less intensity than before. "It was just as much a lie then as it is now. When a boy lies about his mother, he deserves a good whipping. I was right to do what I did."

It was now clear why the Chief had beaten Grandpa with his cane on that long-ago day in the little cemetery, the day my dad decided to leave Climer for good. The beating was a means of salving the old man's conscience. Had he accepted what Grandpa revealed, it would have meant that the vicious treatment of his son had not only been cruel, but totally unjustified. Continuing the abuse was easier than admitting to nearly half a century of misguided hatred and revenge.

"I wonder why Mother never told us what really happened?" Inez said.

Julia had pulled a tissue from her dress pocket, dabbing at her reddened nose. "Because she was so sick over what she had done, and because she knew her husband would never forgive her for what happened."

Anger filled the Chief once again.

"I wouldn't have held that against her. I worshiped that woman."

"Think, Poppa," Julia said. "Momma had to choose between facing you or sacrificing her other son and spending the rest of her life being eaten up with guilt. How afraid of you she must have been to make the choice she did. It must have broken her heart each time she heard you say something bad about Johnny, when she knew full well how noble a boy he was."

Inez leaned against the yellow tulip wallpaper, as if she might faint at any second. "What terrible things to discover about our parents so late in life. This must be a nightmare."

"Yes, a nightmare," agreed Julia. "But only a short one for us. Johnny has been living one for fifty-four years. It has cost him everything. I want you to go to him, Poppa, and invite him to the meeting. You said the other night that it would be a time of new beginnings, and I want you to prove it. You owe it to him."

The Chief clenched his teeth. "I don't owe anybody anything." He shuffled despondently to the stairs and began climbing.

Julia followed him to the bottom step.

"Then I'm going to bring him, Poppa. Or else I'll stay home myself."

"The same here," said Inez.

The Chief did not bother to answer, but continued his painfully slow ascent of the stairs. He looked as old and tired as that day with me in the little cemetery. I had felt sorry for him then; I didn't now.

MISSOURI

*I*t was a Saturday morning in August, 1961—a day to remember forever. It was the day that concluded my search for old silver. It was the day Reverend Daniel Brady came to town and conquered many of Climer's infidels. Most importantly, it was the day that marked a drastic turning point in my existence. It was the last day of my life to be spent in darkness, the last day an empty spot would dwell within me. It was the last day before a glorious new dawn!

Had I judged Saturday's prospects by how things looked at breakfast, I might have been tempted to return to bed and pull the covers over my face. Never had a meal at the hotel been so disorganized. Silverware settings were incomplete, butter and jam were left in the kitchen, ham and eggs were cold and greasy, and nobody seemed to care. The aunts looked like they had spent the night pulling boxcars up the side of a mountain. The Chief didn't even bother to come to the table. There was no mention of last night's startling revelation, but unspoken words hung in the air like hovering dragonflies. Only Belle looked as if her sleep had been unaffected by by the confrontation between Julia and the Chief.

I ate as quickly as possible, both to escape the gloom and to get an early start on the treasure hunt. As I left the table, Dad told me to take off work early because Reverend Brady would be here by 4:30. I said this would be my last day at the turkey farm. When he asked me why, I explained that by late morning I would be rich; working would no longer be necessary. He responded with a cynical, "Yeah, yeah." I laughed to myself. A different type of "yeah,

yeah" would escape his lips when I dumped the old silver under his nose.

On my final journey to the turkey farm, the air was much cooler than the past few days. The wind blew briskly, and clouds were full-sailed schooners skimming across blue waters. It was a great day to be alive, and I found myself wondering if Grandpa had ever felt this good. He had been my age when the accident occurred; it was unlikely there were too many pleasant days in his life after that. One morning he was a happy, normal boy; by nightfall his world had been destroyed. A thought struck that maybe a similar fate awaited me. Wasn't it possible that on any given day an event could take place which might ruin a person's life? Hadn't Paul Jamison Kane started out the final twenty-four hours of his existence believing it to be just another day? Hadn't Jimmy Swailes?

The sunlight around me fell victim to a cloud's shadow. My heart grew chilled. What if God was a lunatic like Don Books, grabbing some poor turkey who happened by and executing him in a moment of rage? What if He thrived on human suffering and anguish? Was that why the world was so full of those very things—because He wanted it that way? Such a thought scared me like nothing ever scared me before. I began running toward National Poultry Incorporated, as if it were possible to outrun a frightening question. That was a childish thing to do, but it worked. By the time I reached the front gate, there were only two things left on my mind: to catch my breath and to find that old silver.

●   ●   ●   ●

At first glance I thought Massachusetts had injured himself. He came walking down the road limping, swinging his leg from the hip without bending at the knee. But instead of a pained expression, he wore a ridiculous grin.

"What's wrong with you?" I asked him.

"Just my arthritis flarin' up. You know, arthritis spelled with a T."

When I didn't catch the hint, he reached inside his overalls and pulled out the top of the tool he had mentioned yesterday. It was made of two iron rods the thickness of my little finger. The cross-piece was about a foot long; the shaft extended from just underneath Massachusetts' chin to somewhere inside his sock. He told me he had put the thing under his clothes to keep Cricketts and Spriggs from getting suspicious.

"Won't they get suspicious anyway if all of a sudden you're walking like a pegleg?"

"Yeah, maybe yer right."

We made a quick trip to the site of my second unsuccessful digging. Massachusetts extracted the tool from his clothing and laid it beside the refilled hole. After morning chores we would begin the final phase of Operation Old Silver.

On my way back to the sheds, Cricketts pulled up beside me in his truck.

"How you doin' there, young Kane?"

"Pretty good."

"Attaboy. Say, I wanted to ask if you was the one that dug that crater out there in the graveyard?"

"Sure did."

"Well for heaven's sake, son, you didn't have to make a hole that big for the few dead birds we get this time of year."

"I know that, Cricketts, but I figured since you were short a man, and since I'm going to have to quit after this morning, that I would dig a little extra so you wouldn't have to worry about it for a while."

The boss gave me a gap-toothed grin worthy of a Halloween pumpkin.

"Doggone if that ain't a nice thing for a guy to do. I appreciate it, an' I'm sorry to hear you're leavin' because you done good for me while you was here. I won't never forget how you put the whammy on old Books with them maggots—no sir, I won't. Course, the worst thing about you leavin' is that I won't get to see you no more because I'm headin' out right now for Kansas City an' won't get back till late. We'll miss you, son."

He offered his hand, then started to calculate my wages. Since money would no longer be of any importance, I told him to forget about it. He insisted I take something for my time. After several minutes of good-natured arguing, he forced me to accept ten dollars as a token payment. When his green pickup disappeared in its own dust storm, I realized Bob C. Ricketts had been a good man to work for. A small stab of guilt penetrated to the core of my conscience for having deceived him throughout the entire time of my employment.

After a hurried, sloppy job of feeding, I went to find Massachusetts. He and Spriggs were repairing fence on the range. We gave a phony excuse to cover our exit, then left Spriggs pounding U-shaped nails into fenceposts. Massachusetts took the Minneapolis-Moline to the treasure site. Fortunately for me the ride was a short one, because he drove like a drunken *kamikaze*. We almost went through the barbed-wire boundary fence before he got the tractor stopped.

"Needs new brakes," he said.

"New driver wouldn't hurt either."

I jumped down from my seat on the fender and picked up the T. "Show me how this thing works."

Massachusetts stepped off the tractor, removing the tool from my hands with an air of disdain.

"This old girl is used to a master's touch, kid. Ain't no amateur alive can make her work. Gimme room."

He rolled his sleeves past the elbows and took a firm grip on the top of the T. After examining yesterday's digging, he placed the point of the tool about a yard to the left and shoved it into the ground.

"Nothin' there," he said.

Two more attempts were unsuccessful. By then I was glad he had talked me into doing it his way; otherwise we might have been digging all day.

Finally my partner probed the area directly in front of the old hole. The rod sunk down a couple feet before hitting something solid.

"Is that it?" I yelled.

"Don't know yet. Let me keep pokin'."

Massachusetts moved the T a few inches at a time, trying to get an idea of how big the obstruction was. After several dozen thrusts, he was certain of the dimensions. With his pocketknife he cut a rough outline into the ground.

"That might be what we're lookin' for, kid."

My hands trembled as I started digging. Nervous anticipation sapped my strength. My arms felt weak, but that didn't matter. If the third time was truly a charm, this hole would be my last.

Just past knee-deep, my spade struck something. A surge of adrenalin gave me the power to dig faster. I concentrated on finding an edge and digging around it. The object was made of wood—some sort of chest or crate. Massachusetts was bent over, peering into the hole.

"That's been down there a while, kid. I bet it's yer uncle's treasure box."

I scooped away the remaining dirt, then stepped out of the hole. We laid down in the grass and tried to pull the prize from its hiding-place. It wouldn't budge.

"Want me to dig some?" asked Massachusetts.

"Nah, I'm okay."

Okay? I was great. My muscles were ready for anything. I could have dug up the underground vaults at Fort Knox. In less than a minute I had enlarged the sides of the hole enough to allow the wooden chest to be extracted. Ever so carefully we lifted it to higher ground. Our prize looked as if it might disintegrate should someone sneeze. How ironic that a valuable treasure would be stored inside such a pitiful container. We stood over it, impatient yet hesitant, confident yet unsure.

"There's a hammer in the toolbox," said Massachusetts in a trancelike tone.

I ran to the tractor and brought back a hammer and a pair of pliers. Small, rusted nails held the rotting boards together. Some of them were loose, protruding just enough for the pliers to pinch. When I pulled the first nail out, the contents of the chest made a chinking sound. Silver coins sliding across one another would produce just such a sound. My brain was in danger of shorting out; my heart pounded like a jackhammer.

"The old mouth's waterin' like a hog in a cornfield," admitted Massachusetts.

My own mouth was dry. There wasn't enough saliva in it to dissolve a sugar granule. But the only important thing was getting the chest opened. I removed another nail and felt the board come loose. A stiff yank with the claws of the hammer popped it off. Two more boards were easily torn away. The top was now completely open. Inside the chest was a tattered burlap sack. It held the treasure that Lathom Kane had buried, the treasure I had pursued these past days, the treasure that would provide me with all the things a guy could ever want. I cut the sack.

The glittering contents spilled into the grass, catching the sun's rays and reflecting them back at us. Slivers of rainbow shimmered against my faded jeans.

"Look at that," whispered a stunned Massachusetts. "Just look."

To look was the only thing I was capable of doing. As had happened so often the past two weeks, my body quit working. My arms and legs felt as dead as General Lee's horse; my voice was inaudible. Only the eyes continued to function. What they saw were countless pieces of glass in a variety of shapes and sizes. The sack had been full of broken bottles!

"I think we been bamboozled, kid," said Massachusetts, picking up one of the larger fragments that had some sort of a label stuck to it.

"This can't be it," I croaked. "This chest just happened to be buried out here too. It's a coincidence."

"I don't think so."

He held out the piece of glass so I could read the faded writing on the label. The first word to catch my eye was "whiskey." Then I saw something that almost made me cry. In fancy lettering, beneath a small picture of a full-bearded man, were the words "OLD SILVER."

"I don't believe this," I said, slumping to the ground. "Why would a guy bury some stinking broken bottles and call it a treasure?"

"Well, if I remember how ya told it to me, I don't know that he ever exactly said it was a treasure. All he said was he buried some old silver."

"But why would he bury broken bottles?"

"They probably wasn't busted when he buried 'em, kid. My guess is that moisture got into the chest over the years an' collected in the bottom. Then one winter them bottles just started crackin' an' bustin'. But long as they been layin' out here, it coulda been anything that broke 'em. Maybe some alcoholic worms went on a toot, who knows?"

Massachusetts was probably right, and I had to face facts. Prior to entering the hospital, Lathom Kane had buried his most valuable possessions: half a dozen bottles of a cheap whiskey named Old Silver. He did this so his wife wouldn't drink it all before he came back. The cache remained untouched until years later when an idiot discovered a diary in which the insignificant burial was recorded. That same idiot went to great lengths and deceived many in an attempt to recover a chest of broken glass. Now he had gotten a bellyful of the whole business and was ready to slink home to lick his wounds. He got up off the ground.

"I'm leaving, Massachusetts."

"Figgered you would be. Ain't nothin' here for a kid like you if there ain't no treasure to be diggin'."

"I'll help you clean up this mess first."

"No need. Just a matter of tossin' the junk back in the hole an' fillin' it up again. I'll get it later on."

I stood there trying to think of the right words for a man who had become a favorite of mine. I shook his hand.

"Sorry I led you on a goose chase, Massachusetts. I really thought I was on to something good."

"Don't you be worryin' about that none. I had me more fun the last two days than I had the whole time I been here. You ever get back this way again, look me up. Maybe we'll invite old Booksie over an' fry us up a mess of maggots. Take care, kid."

With that said, Massachusetts Conlon Rodgers walked back to the tractor, started it, and drove toward the range. When he was out of sight, I turned away from the shattered fragments that had been my dream and left National Poultry Incorporated for the final time. I had been there only four days, but it seemed forever. Twice forever. The turkeys, the buildings, the slop, the smells, and all the unusual people working at that place had become a part of my world simply because once upon a time a drunk buried some bottles. If that didn't prove life was absurd, nothing ever would!

• • • •

The little cemetery was no longer a place of strangers to me. I was familiar with many of them by now: Eleanor Kane, Lathom

Kane, Paul Jamison Kane. It was only fair that I know something of them because they had in different ways been affecting me since the day I was born. Who could measure the impact upon my life of Eleanor Kane's actions of fifty-four years ago? If she had not wrecked that wagon, if she had told the truth after it happened, the resulting difference in Grandpa's life and later in Dad's life and still later in my own life would have been incalculable. How incredible that the deeds of one person could influence people born into future generations.

Seeing Lathom Kane's grave reminded me that God was a con artist, no better than the blonde at the carnival. What a fool I had been for Him. Like a performing seal in a circus, I had done His tricks and swallowed every fish He threw my way. I had believed in His signs and promises, but they were as worthless as the treasure He provided. I knew now, without a doubt, that God was cruel. He was a sneaky, double-talking troublemaker who killed young boys and broke old people's hearts. I hated Him and burned inside at the pain He had caused me and my family across the years.

The more I thought about it, the madder I became. I began muttering to myself what a bum He was. Soon I was talking out loud, shouting obscenities at the heavens. I shook my fist and called Him every filthy name my ears had ever heard. When the list was exhausted, I began to innovate. I combined cuss words; I split them and inserted others between the parts. I prefixed and suffixed them to His name. I profaned all that existed above the clouds and below them, and every fish in the deep blue sea. I cursed the living, the dead, and those individuals who floated somewhere in the mid-dle—like Dracula and Mrs. Murphy, my sixth grade math teacher. I was a human volcano spewing verbal lava, hoping to darken the white robes of the angels with the black ashes of my soul.

Later, when my anger was spent, silence returned to the ceme-tery. The only sound to be heard was the whine of passing bees and maybe a low rumble beneath the grass. This could have been noth-ing less than my ancestors doing a collective roll within their coffins, or perhaps it was the gates of Hell swinging open to accom-modate the inevitable entrance of one so foolish as to do what I had just done. But who cared? At least God knew what I really thought of Him and His practical jokes. Cussing Him out wasn't much of a way to gain revenge, but what could a guy do? Outside of burning down a church or sticking gum between the pages of a Bible, I couldn't think of any action that would be effective against an invisible enemy living in Heaven. All I could do now was to completely ignore Him and anybody who tried to say good things about Him. That included the Reverend Daniel Brady, who was due at the hotel in a matter of hours.

• • • •

What a difference half a day made. The confusion and apathy witnessed at breakfast had been replaced by organization and enthusiasm. The aunts were everywhere at once—cleaning, polishing, and preparing food. Mom assisted them, while Dad cut grass and trimmed the lilac bushes. The Chief was in the middle of everything, but seemed to be proceeding with caution. He didn't issue orders, but politely asked if this could be taken care of or if that could be done. Occasionally he attempted a humorous remark, to which the aunts responded with perfunctory smiles. It was clear that the ladies were making preparations to honor their guest, not their father. A gap had developed in the relationship that would not easily be bridged.

A little past 2 I decided to take a quick bath, only to discover Belle still occupying her favorite spot in the hotel. Since my return from the little cemetery nearly two hours earlier, she had yet to yield one minute of bathroom time. I tried slipping away undetected, but my poor luck continued.

"Aren't we speaking today?"

"I figured you were busy."

"I see." She sniffed in my direction. "You need a bath, little man."

"Somebody's always in the bathroom."

"That's odd, I never seem to have any trouble getting in." She laughed and began running a comb through her black hair. "Are you planning on going forward tonight?"

"Forward where?"

"At the gospel meeting, you twit. After the sermon is over, the preacher will ask for people to come up front and get saved. It's the way they usually wrap up an affair like this. Sort of makes it all official."

Saved? There was that word again, the same one Jimmy had used just before the accident. Was a similar fate about to descend upon Belle? At least then I would be able to get into the bathroom.

"What do people get out of going forward?" I asked.

"Oh, I suppose that depends on the individual. Some might do it to clear a guilty conscience, and some might do it to impress a certain person."

I had the feeling that she was telling me something. "Are you thinking about doing it?"

"Let's just say that in the last twenty-four hours a lot of people have given the Chief reason to cross their names off his list. If I'm a good little girl, I might move up to the top spot before that preacher leaves town. And if I put on a convincing enough show when I go up front, I might even get a star beside my name. A gold star!"

"But would you really be saved?"

"You bet I would, kiddo. Anything that increases my bankroll enough to get me out of this dump will be a salvation. This little Belle longs to chime in some beautiful tower, but beautiful towers cost money." She closed the door. "I'll be out in five minutes."

"I'll believe that when I see it."

Rather than waste any more time waiting for her, I went upstairs to dig out some decent clothes. Flipping through dresser drawers, I made a vow never to be like Belle and let money dictate my life. Such a high-minded resolution left me feeling quite superior to her; then I remembered that my last four days had been spent skulking around a turkey farm in search of riches. Perhaps we were two of a kind. But no, there was a difference. There were certain things I would not do for monetary gain, one of them being that business about going forward at the gospel meeting. Never would I do that—not for silver, not for anything. Belle could get saved if she thought it might do her some good. She could tap dance up the aisle singing "Hound Dog" for all I cared. But there would be no such shenanigans for me. I had already been involved in one of God's crooked deals, and that was plenty!

• • • •

I was mentally prepared to meet the Reverend Daniel Brady, and I knew exactly what kind of man he would be. He would be old and ugly and grim. He would wear black clothes and say "thee" and "thou" instead of talking like a normal person. He would refer to everyone as "brother" or "sister" and would know absolutely nothing about any subject of importance to me. I could be certain of all this because every preacher I had met or seen on television fit that description. What puzzled me was whether those characteristics were necessary to get the job or were simply the result of having gotten the job. Either way, it seemed a sorry existence.

The hall clock had just struck half past 4 when I saw a green Volkswagen pull into the driveway. A handsome, younger man with blond, almost-white hair stepped out. He wore a pullover sport shirt and gray slacks. I thought him to be a salesman or a stranger in need of directions. I was wrong.

"He's here," Julia called from the kitchen.

The Chief went shuffling past the dining room doorway. Inez was right behind him. Mom and Dad hurried down the stairs and followed the crowd out back to meet our guest. I remained at the window to watch the introductions.

"I hope this is where the Kane family lives," said the man, flashing an effortless smile at the Chief as they shook hands.

"Reverend Daniel Brady, I presume," said the Chief.

"Yes, sir. I'm pleased to meet you and these lovely ladies."

As the Chief introduced the aunts and my parents, Belle made a dramatic entrance into the dining room. It was wasted on me.

"Oh! Where are they at?"

"Outside, but I think they're getting ready to come in."

"How do I look?" she asked as footsteps sounded in the kitchen.

"Good."

That wasn't quite true; she looked better than good. Her hair was perfect, and her makeup was flawless. It could have been a real face. She wore a dark-blue skirt with a frilly white blouse and a wide silver belt that matched her earrings. At that moment she almost looked beautiful, but in sort of an evil way, like the wicked queen in "Snow White."

The Chief led the procession into the dining room. Everyone was talking, but Reverend Brady's attention seemed to be upon the furnishings.

"Mr. Kane, your home is magnificent."

"Thank you, sir. We try to keep it nice, but it's almost too much for us now. It used to be a hotel, you know."

"Did it really? I bet there are a lot of memories inside these old walls."

"If you only knew," said Belle, showing her best haughty smile.

Reverend Brady noticed us for the first time, seemingly surprised that more family members remained to be greeted. He looked to the Chief for an introduction.

"My granddaughter Belle and my great-grandson Thomas Jamison Kane," said the Chief. His flat tone of voice and unenthused manner indicated our second-class status. We were a couple of pits in his bowl of fresh cherries.

"Belle . . ." said Reverend Brady. "That's a beautiful name."

"Isn't it though," she said. "Thank goodness I've been able to live up to it."

Everyone chuckled at the remark, but only the preacher's laughter sounded genuine. Then he reached for my hand. I noticed that his bicep rippled at the slightest movement, and his muscular forearm was covered with thick yellow fuzz. His palm swallowed mine.

"Thomas Jefferson, was it?"

"Tom is fine."

"Glad to meet you, Tom. Say, I bet you're a ballplayer of some kind, aren't you?"

"Uh, yeah, I like baseball."

"Hey, great. That's my favorite sport. Since this is Missouri, I bet you're a St. Louis Cardinals fan and your favorite player is Stan Musial. Right?"

"Actually we live in Iowa, and I'm a Yankee fan. My favorite player is Mickey Mantle."

A look of delight crossed the preacher's face; he laughed out loud.

"Hallelujah . . . I've found another Yankee-lover. We must be the only two west of the Mississippi. Tell you what, after we eat let's get together for a few minutes and talk some baseball. Okay?"

"Sure!"

Before anything else could be said, the Chief took hold of Reverend Brady's arm and steered him away from me.

"We might as well see the rest of the hotel while we wait on dinner," he said, staring an icy hole through my skull.

"I'd love to," said the guest.

Julia and Inez went to the kitchen as the others moved toward the lobby. I decided to stay put and avoid the rush. The Chief was already giving background information on the grandfather clock. Should supper be late, Reverend Brady would end up knowing the history of every piece of furniture in the building.

"You certainly stole that scene," Belle said after the room emptied.

"Huh?"

"Don't play dumb with me, little fool. I know a leech when I see one. How dare you waste that man's valuable time with your mindless prattle."

"All I did was talk about baseball."

"All you did was get in my way and sink your hooks into that poor man. Do you honestly think he can afford to clog his mind with something as idiotic as baseball? He was just being polite, in case you hadn't figured it out. I suggest you keep your mouth shut from now on and let the adults have a chance to get to know him."

She whirled and left the room to join the Chief's tour. Soon I heard outbursts of her phony laughter over the buzz of voices. Later, when the group had migrated to the parlor, I thought it was Belle who played several snappy tunes on the piano. But in the middle of a song she came back into the dining room and flopped onto a chair.

"Who's playing the piano?" I asked her.

"Mr. Wonderful, the Reverend Daniel Beethoven. Or so he thinks."

"No kidding? Then I guess you were right the other day."

"About what?"

"About men playing the piano. He plays, and he sure ain't no sissy."

"I think he's a musclebound fairy," she said, jumping up and heading out again. "And his choice of music is rather common, if you ask me."

I went to the parlor to catch the tail end of the preacher's performance. His piano playing appeared as smooth as everything else he did. The man certainly was unusual. How could such a young, handsome, and talented guy, a Yankee fan to boot, be a preacher? He just didn't fit the part.

A nervous anticipation began swirling the juices inside my stomach. The feeling was not unlike the one I had experienced while opening the wooden chest, and yet there was a difference. It was more like what I felt that first afternoon at the hotel lying on the brass bed and reading the inscription inside Jimmy's ring. Now, as then, something told me I was on the edge of some great discovery, some new ground my feet had never trodden, some rarefied air my lungs had yet to breathe. It was as if a gorgeous bubble had just floated past my face, compelling me to give chase. Now, as then, I told myself such feelings made no sense whatsoever. No more than a blond-haired, piano-playing, baseball-loving preacher.

• • • •

Throughout the evening meal I watched Reverend Daniel Brady from a distant vantage point. The Chief sat in his customary spot at the head of the table, with our guest of honor to his immediate right. Belle and I occupied similar positions at the opposite end. The seating arrangement seemed designed to keep heretics and lunatics on the fringe, where their words might have the least effect.

Reverend Brady appeared completely relaxed in a roomful of strangers. He treated the Chief with respect, but showed none of the nervousness or intimidation exhibited by most people in the old man's presence. He was the only person I ever heard call my great-grandfather "Oliver." His manners and speech hinted that he came from the upper classes; yet I got the impression that he knew the heart of the common man very well.

Bit by bit he gave us glimpses of his life: born and raised in Framingham, Massachusetts; educated at Holy Cross; married a girl named Maria; spent two years on the Nigerian mission field; was called into a full-time evangelistic ministry in 1957.

"Who did this call come from?" Belle asked him, trying hard to look sincere.

"A true calling comes from God," he explained.

"Well, as a former switchboard operator with many years of experience, I would like to know how to plug in a call from God. I've never seen it done."

Eyebrows raised all around the table, and I could tell by the Chief's expression that he wished he had seated Belle in the garage. But Reverend Brady showed a confident grin.

"I'm lucky, Belle. When my Boss wants to get hold of someone, He doesn't need a switchboard. He communicates person to person, twenty-four hours a day, anywhere on the planet."

"Does He always get through?"

"No . . . Sometimes He gets a busy signal, and sometimes the other party refuses to answer."

"And then?"

"Oh, He'll keep trying for quite a while, but there comes a point in time when He has to disconnect. But the charges still have to be paid, if you know what I mean."

Belle must have understood that this man would be more than a match for her in a battle of wits, because she merely nodded her approval of his answer. Nothing more was heard from her until the main course had been finished and the dishes cleared away.

For dessert we had peach ice cream, made by the Chief, just like our first day at the hotel. Reverend Brady pleased the old man by saying it was the best he had ever tasted. "You will have to give my wife the recipe," he said, "unless it's a family secret."

Maria Brady was at that moment attending a conference of church women called to go over last-minute details of the gospel meeting. She would eat at the church and afterward walk the two blocks to the hotel to spend some time with us.

"I wish your wife could have been here for supper," Inez said for the third time.

"Duty before pleasure, sister," said Julia. "We must all do our share. Normally we would have been at the conference too, but our duty was to be here tonight."

"Why, Aunt Julia," said Belle, feigning shock, "are you saying that serving Reverend Brady is a duty rather than a pleasure?"

Julia blushed the quickest, deepest blush I ever saw.

"Oh, my goodness, no! Dear Reverend Brady, I hope you didn't take it that way."

"Of course I didn't, Julia. I've been in enough homes and met enough people to know true hospitality from an imitation. You and Inez are delightful hostesses. I wish I had it this good everywhere I preach."

The post-meal conversation continued another half-hour. Reverend Brady finally stood up.

"Oliver," he said, "if you don't mind, I think I'll stretch my legs a bit. Maybe Tom could walk me around the block once or twice."

"I thought you would like to rest before the meeting," said the Chief.

"Sometimes I find that a little exercise is more restful than rest."

"Suit yourself. Go with him, Thomas Jamison."

"Yes, sir!"

I was afraid Fred would ask to go along, but we made it out the door with no escort. We cut across the side yard toward Main Street. Remembering how pitiful the town had looked to me that first day, I couldn't help wondering how much worse it must seem to a man as worldly as him.

"Ain't much of a place, is it," I said.

"It isn't big, if that's what you mean. But it has the one thing I'm always looking for."

"What could that possibly be?"

"People who are hurting, people who have needs that aren't being met."

"Like who?"

"Well, I can't name names because we just got here, but this little town and the surrounding area is sure to have its share of drunks, bums, lonely people, sickly people, widows, juvenile delinquents, and all the rest."

"Heck yes . . . Our family has most of those categories all by itself."

He laughed. "Then I came to the right place, didn't I?"

"Guess so." I wanted to say something, but didn't know how to bring it up. He sensed my dilemma.

"Tell me."

"Pardon?"

"Tell me the question that's dangling off the end of your tongue."

"It might make you mad."

"Me get mad at a Yankee fan? Never happen."

"All right then . . . This morning I cussed out God and decided not to have anything more to do with Him or the gospel meeting tonight. Or even with you."

He looked at me with amused curiosity.

"Why would you do that?"

"I got tired of Him always messing me up."

"How does He mess you up?"

"Well, He keeps promising that something will work out good, and then it doesn't."

We were passing the Climer Cafe. The air around us was full of the smell of chili and pie. Reverend Brady walked with his head down, hands clasped behind his back. "How did He make those promises known to you?"

"By flipping a coin."

"You mean heads and tails, that sort of thing?"

"Yep."

He put a hand over his eyes and shook his head in mock dismay. "Tell me I'm dreaming."

"What's wrong with doing it that way?"

The preacher threw an arm across my shoulders as we walked, like he'd known me for years. I liked that.

"How did you ever get started on this coin business?"

"Well, this one day I was trying to decide if there was a God. So I told Him to give me a sign if He was real. Right then I found a quarter in the grass, and I started using it to find out what was going to happen."

"Only it didn't work out, did it?"

"No. I thought it was going to, but it didn't. That means I'm an idiot, I guess."

"Hardly," he said. "It just means that you're one of those people

I mentioned—the ones whose needs aren't being met. Your particular need is to find out what God really wants you to do without resorting to something like flipping a coin. It's possible you could learn something about that at the meeting tonight, if you decide to come."

"I'll probably have to come, but I won't like it."

"Just give it a fair chance, that's all I ask. And one more thing . . ."

"What?"

"Don't ask God for proof that He exists and then insult him by accepting something as silly as a quarter lying in the grass. Ask for something tough, something unmistakable that only He could do. If He's real, nothing will be too difficult."

That made sense, and I kept those words in the back of my mind even as we talked about other things. By the time we got back to the hotel, I knew exactly what I would ask God to do. We were on the front porch, and I was about to inform Reverend Brady of my decision when a woman's voice called from behind us.

"Dan, wait a minute."

A dark-haired female in a sleeveless beige dress waved from across the street.

"It's my wife. I want you to meet her."

As the woman walked toward us, head down and hurrying, I saw she had a beautiful tan. Her hair was so dark that there was almost a hint of blue. It reminded me of someone else's hair, but I couldn't think whose.

"Tom Kane," said the preacher as his wife climbed the porch steps, "this is the lovely, enchanting Maria Brady."

She lifted her face to me for the first time, and I noticed three things at once: her teeth were good enough to be in a Colgate commercial, her earrings were small crosses, and she was a Mexican!

"Pleased to meet you, Tom Kane," she said, extending her hand. There was the slightest trace of an accent.

"Yeah, sure." I ignored her hand, moving backward a couple of steps. I imagined the sound of a faraway siren floating on the warm breeze. The form of Jimmy Swailes, bloodied and still, lay before me in the street. Maria Brady's smile faded; she looked to her husband for an explanation. He had none

"Is something wrong, Tom?" he asked.

I stared into the woman's face and remembered a drunken sneer. I remembered a shack at twilight and dropping a Mexican kid with one swing of a paint can. Most of all, I remembered a small body in a blue suit lying inside a casket.

"I don't feel too good," I said, turning away from them and walking into the lobby. They followed, calling my name, but I went upstairs and shut the bedroom door.

The gospel meeting was due to start in ninety minutes.

MISSOURI

A little before 7 I heard someone in the hall. Mom opened the door.

"Here you are! We've been wondering where you went. The Bradys have already left, and we'll be leaving in a few minutes. You better get your good clothes on."

"I'm not going."

"Of course you are."

"No way, Mom. I've decided, and that's it."

She pulled a clean pair of socks from the dresser drawer and sailed them past my head. They bounced off the vanity mirror. Her eyes were narrow.

"You get changed, and be quick about it. We've got enough tension around this place without you creating more. You've got five minutes."

The door slammed. I began changing clothes, but with the same enthusiasm as one who readies himself for the gallows. I felt depressed and tired. I was homesick. I wanted to go back to McKinley and sleep in my own bed. I wanted to shoot baskets with Hippo. Instead, I was headed for some hick church to listen to a preacher and his Mexican wife talk about how wonderful God was. I would rather have done anything else, even dig another hole in the turkey farm graveyard. At least I knew how bad that would be.

By the time I got downstairs, the rest of the family had gathered on the front sidewalk. I fell into line at the rear of the parade, along with Belle. She now wore a light blue dress with white shoes and a matching purse.

"The Chief isn't pleased with you," she said. "He wanted to leave five minutes ago."

"Big deal."

"Well, my my . . . I assumed you would want to get there just as soon as you could to spend a few extra minutes with that preacher man."

"No thanks."

She put her hand to her mouth in mock dismay.

"Don't tell me there's trouble in paradise! Young Master Thomas finally figured out what Miss Belle knew all along: that the Reverend Daniel Brady is nothing but a sweet-talking phony. He had all of you eating out of his hand. By the time he left here he could have said Eisenhower was still president and everyone would have gone along with it. It's a good thing he was only here for one afternoon."

"Why?"

"Because a smooth talker like him could have ended up with everything we owned and left us standing in just our choir robes. If you think you got fleeced at that carnival, little lamb, think what that man could have done with a week of your time."

"Do you really think he's a phony?"

"Everybody's a phony, dear boy, but some people conceal it better than others. Now watch out . . . I want to get up there by dear old Chiefy and tell him how wonderful it is having Reverend Brady here tonight. Ta-ta."

• • • •

I had seen the little church dozens of times before, or at least ones very similar. It was the kind always seen in the movies, on calendars, and in Rockwell prints. It was a white, woodframe structure with a spired steeple housing a bell. Ancient oaks provided a blanket of shade. Above the main entrance was the inscription, "Climer Baptist—Erected 1904."

Except for parked cars, the scene before me could have been any Sunday evening from fifty-seven years ago when the church was new. I visualized the buggies and wagons of those days. The Chief, with dark hair and a jaunty step, would be walking his young family over from the hotel. Paul Jamison Kane would still be alive; Grandpa would be just a little older than Fred.

Grandpa! In the confusion of the day I had forgotten him. Nobody had said whether or not he was coming, but the presence of Julia and Inez indicated there was a possibility. As we approached the front steps I looked around for his Chevy wagon, but didn't see it.

What I did see was Reverend Brady. The preacher now wore a gray suit and a blue tie. As we entered, he was there to shake hands and say a few words in passing. When my turn came, he handed me a quarter.

"Here . . . If I don't teach you anything tonight, you'll need this."

He gave me that grin of his, making it clear we were still friends despite what had happened earlier. I took the coin and gave his hand the tightest squeeze I could produce. He was an all-right guy.

The sanctuary of the church contained a pulpit, a piano, and two sections of pews. Each pew was well-polished, but the wood underneath the shine was nicked and timeworn. We sat on the right side. The Chief was on the end; then came Belle, Inez, Mom, and Fred. Another family occupied the rest of the space, so Dad, Julia, and I sat one row back. The Chief and Belle were directly in front of me. My scheming cousin had been careful to get next to the old man so he could get a close look at whatever she was going to do. Unfortunately I would also be forced to witness her performance.

There were still ten minutes before the scheduled starting time, but the building was nearly full. The crowd had a distinctly rural appearance. Many red-faced farmers were dressed in overalls, and some looked in need of a clean shirt. Dirty boots had left their mark upon the floor. A few older men wore more traditional church garb, while most of the ladies seemed to have chosen the best their closets had to offer. Despite cooler weather, the air around us became uncomfortable as sour armpits made their presence known.

I had only been inside a church once before, for Good Friday services. All I remembered was a fat lady singing a hymn filled with falsetto notes, and a minister droning on forever in multisyllabled words which meant no more to me than the national anthem of Tibet. One woke the dead, one put me to sleep. Both seemed a sorry waste of time.

"Think an' explodin' cracker'd wake this place up a little?"

I looked around and saw Grandpa standing in the aisle. He had on a brown suit that might have fit a man four inches taller and fifty pounds heavier. His maroon tie had yellow palm trees stitched across the lower half. Julia stood up and leaned over me to hug him.

"We're so happy you came, Johnny."

"Almost didn't make it. Had a pint of whiskey that wanted me to stay home and howl at the moon, but I came anyway. How ya been there, Tomcat?"

"Pretty good," I said.

"Attaboy. Hello, Junior—how ya like my duds?"

"You look great, Dad," lied my father. "Sit down here between Julia and me."

"Well, I appreciate that, but I'd rather stay back at the door in case I need to get some air. Just came up to tell ya hello."

The rest of the family turned around to greet Grandpa, all except for the Chief. He was talking to the people in the pew ahead of him, and made a point to continue doing so until his son left.

Finally Maria Brady emerged from a door behind the pulpit. All conversation ceased. The preacher's wife had a guitar strapped over her shoulder. The large instrument made her appear small, but she spoke with a strong voice which easily carried to us.

"We would like to thank you all for coming out tonight. I will begin the evening with a song of praise entitled 'How Great Thou Art.'"

She began strumming the guitar and sang in a manner which could only be described as beautiful, regardless of any prejudices a guy might have against one of her kind. Even though she was singing, it seemed she was uttering a prayer:

"O Lord, my God, when I in awesome wonder consider all the worlds Thy hands have made, I see the stars . . ."

As soon as I heard her mention stars, I thought of Grandpa. Hadn't he said almost the same thing the night of his birthday—that seeing the stars made him realize there must be a God? His method of expression was crude compared to Maria's, but the content was similar. Maybe there was something significant about that.

Applause brought my wandering mind back to the service. Maria smiled at the crowd as she began another hymn. This one was more lively, and some of the people clapped their hands to the beat. Heads in front of me oscillated in varied patterns of rhythmic interpretation. Only the Chief appeared unaffected by the music.

After the second hymn, Maria took time to thank the Women's Auxiliary for its efforts at the conference supper; she also thanked the Kane family for taking such good care of her husband. The crowd applauded again. The Chief acknowledged them by nodding his head, as if it was all for him.

Ushers went to the front and passed collection plates down each pew. The one that came our way contained mostly change with a couple of wrinkled bills looking lonesome and out of place. I contributed the quarter Reverend Brady had given me. Such an act might have been a statement of faith in what I was about to hear; it might also have been an attempt to avoid looking like a cheapskate.

When the money had been gathered, Maria sang one more hymn—"When the Roll Is Called Up Yonder." She sang with great forcefulness and put the guitar through quite a workout. At first I paid more attention to her style than to the words she sang, but soon the message began to touch me. The hymn spoke of a day when there would be a roll call in Heaven. Maria said that when the names were called off, she would be there to answer the roll. Her powerful delivery of those words almost made me believe that she had some special assurance for the future. I wished the same could be said for myself and Grandpa and the rest of us. We were undoubtedly listed in lower places—hotter places.

As the echoes of approval for Maria's final hymn faded, Reverend Daniel Brady walked to the pulpit. There was silence inside the church as he adjusted his notes in front of him. Outside, the two-toned whine of locusts signaled the onset of dusk.

"WHERE IS YOUR TREASURE?"

His voice shattered the quiet like a rock shatters cheap glass. Not only did the suddenness and the volume of it startle me, but the very question itself was a shock. I felt my face burning. How had he found out about the treasure? That darn Massachusetts must have spilled his guts, and somehow the story got back to the preacher.

"Two thousand years ago Jesus Christ said, 'Where your treasure is, there will your heart be also.' So I'm asking each of you here tonight to consider where your treasure is—where your heart is."

I breathed a sigh of relief; his question had not been specifically directed at me. It was a good one though, and I was curious to hear more.

"Jesus asked another question. He asked the people of his time, 'What does it profit a man to gain the world and lose his own soul?' Twenty centuries later I ask the same thing. What good will it do anyone here tonight to spend their life pursuing the world's pleasures—the money, the power, the possessions, the beautiful people—if the cost of attaining those items is your own immortal soul?"

A few of the crowd murmured, "Amen."

"WHAT is your treasure? If you desire eternal life, your gold must be God and your precious gem must be Jesus Christ. Jesus said, 'Lay not up for yourselves treasures upon earth, where moth and rust doth corrupt, and where thieves break through and steal.' Think about it, people. Your earthly treasures are at this very minute in the process of disintegration. Your dollar is worth less than ever before, your possessions are older than ever before, your body is closer to death than ever before, and yet you cling to them like a child clings to a favorite toy. Why? Your treasures cannot buy you one more second of life. They cannot save you from death. In many cases they do just the opposite and move you closer to destruction. The lure of treasure will lead you into places you would never have gone otherwise."

Reverend Brady's last sentence hit me like a fist in the stomach. All I had to do was picture myself shoulder-deep in a turkey graveyard, with cotton stuffed up my nose and a handkerchief covering my face, to understand the truth in those words. I thought of Lathom Kane's treasure, pitiful as it was, being destroyed by the passage of time. The broken glass, the rotten, whiskey-stained chest, and the rusted nails were all disintegrating, just like the preacher said. It was almost as if he had the ability to look inside my head and view the events of my life. I found this to be somewhat spooky, albeit enlightening.

The subject of the sermon gradually switched from treasure to sin. We were told emphatically that each one of us was a sinner; nobody was perfect. I was surprised that the Chief didn't take offense at that statement. We were told that everyone was condemned to Hell. Burning, searing, everlasting Hell. Talk about depressing!

As Reverend Brady took a sip of water, I saw people squirming in their seats. Bits of conversation buzzed the pews like flies along a pane of glass. Dad kept shifting his gaze between the ceiling and the floor, as if his eyes could not find a comfortable place to rest. Behind me, standing in the doorway, Grandpa's face was as blank as the last sheet of paper in a new tablet. But just as I was about to ask for my quarter back, things got better.

"That's the bad news, folks. But take heart—I've got good news." The preacher smiled for the first time. "Jesus saves! Hallelujah! God sent Jesus to die for us. It was an act of love which no human can truly understand. The Apostle Paul called Jesus' death an 'unspeakable gift,' and please understand that 'gift' is the appropriate word. Salvation is a gift from God. It cannot be earned, it cannot be bought, it cannot be passed on from one generation to the next. It can only be given. But a gift has no meaning unless it is accepted. Each of you has to reach out and take what God is offering. Will you do that tonight? Will you accept Jesus as Savior?"

I found myself nodding that I would, but stopped as soon as the act became conscious to me. If this was the business of going forward that Belle had mentioned earlier, forget it. I wasn't really sure what was happening here, and the last thing I wanted was to get roped into another of God's farces.

"Don't let pride hold you back. There isn't any other solution to sin. Jesus said, 'I am the way, the truth, and the life:. no man cometh unto the Father, but by me.'"

A shock ran through my body that was equal to the time I shoved a pair of tweezers into an electrical outlet. Even the hair on my arms stood up to salute the Lord. At last I understood that the mysterious words inside Jimmy's ring belonged to Jesus. Those words had been whispering to my heart since the first time I saw them. God had been calling my number, as Reverend Brady had said to Belle during supper, but I hadn't answered. He kept the lines open these past two weeks, waiting in case I changed my mind. Now, as the sermon was concluding, I considered picking up the phone.

"I'm going to ask you to do two things here tonight. First, I want you to empty out your hearts. Open them up and pour out the bitterness, the hatred, the prejudice. If you hold ill feeling toward anyone, let go of it. God is willing to forgive us of all we've done, and we in turn must forgive those who have wronged us."

Again I knew he was speaking directly at me because of my poor behavior toward Maria. Wouldn't he have been shocked to know of the others I had hated? Or did he know already? I concentrated on opening my heart, on letting the poison drain out. It wasn't easy. I could overlook the pain caused me by Dad, the Chief, Don Books, and so many others. I could forgive *them*. Carlos Montez wouldn't be so easy.

"The other thing I want you to do is to come up here and receive God's gift. I want you to do it publicly because when you reach out to God you must not be ashamed. When Christ was nailed to a cross on Calvary Hill, He paid the price of your shame. Don't hold on to it. Don't let Satan tell you that it's too late or that your sins are too great. Jesus' blood covers them all, and this is the day of your deliverance. Walk this aisle to life, my friends. Do it now."

Maria Brady stood up and began playing her guitar. She sang softly, but I wasn't listening to the words. My only thought was of walking to the front and accepting the gift being offered. I wanted to go to Heaven; I wanted forgiveness. But just as I was ready to stand, Belle slid forward in her pew.

"Let me out," she whispered to the Chief. He stared blankly at

her, as if he she were speaking Hebrew, as if his mind were somewhere on the far side of Jupiter.

In an instant my mind changed. I no longer wanted to go forward. If a phony like Belle could still make a game of this, then
maybe a game was all it was.

People were already walking in the aisle. One of them stopped
just in front of me. I looked up and saw a funny-looking little man
in a baggy, brown suit. It was Grandpa. There were tears trailing
down his cheeks. He bent over the Chief.

"I forgive you, Poppa," he said, kissing the old man on the fore-
head. They looked into each other's eyes for several seconds. Then
Grandpa stood straight and walked up the aisle toward Reverend
Brady.

The Chief sat frozen until his son was halfway to the front.
Suddenly he began shaking. His breathing became irregular, and
he gasped for air. I thought he was having a heart attack. In one
way, perhaps he was. Ignoring the concerned inquiries of those
around him, he struggled to his feet.

"Son!" he cried weakly.

That single word, inaudible to most who were there, stopped
my grandfather like a brick wall. He turned around toward us and
was nearly knocked over backward by his father's embrace.

It was a sight I shall never forget: my grandfather and great-
grandfather in each other's arms, in front of most of the town,
weeping, rejoicing, forgiving. People flowed by them on both sides,
like creek waters around a protruding stick, but they were
unaware. The hug was awkward-looking, but after fifty-four years
they were out of practice.

That moment was a wonderful one for them, and also for me.
God had answered my challenge. On the advice of Reverend Brady,
I had asked the Lord to do something big, something so hard that
only He could have done it. I had requested Him to bring Grandpa
and the Chief back together after all those wasted years. Time
couldn't do it, nor could the prompting of loved ones. Even the
truth, revealed after decades of deception, had not been enough.
Only God was capable of restoring the bond between them, and He
had just done it before my wondering eyes. But the miracles
weren't over yet.

Somebody crushed my feet in a clumsy effort to reach the aisle. As the man brushed by me, I expected some word of apology. None came. Dad obviously had other things on his mind. He walked quickly to the front, open-mouthed and wet-faced, to join his elders.

Could anything have touched me more profoundly than seeing my father walk to the front during a church service? I would sooner have believed Julia going forward to do a striptease behind her featherduster. Mom must have felt the same way. She stared after Dad like a zombie in a low-budget movie. Belle's reaction was somewhat different.

"Look at that," she muttered to nobody in particular, "it's a regular fool's parade. I've never seen so many phonies in one line."

Two things were now clear to me: Belle was not going to go forward, and Tom Kane was. Three generations ahead of me were making reservations for eternity; why not make it four?

I must have floated toward the pulpit, because my feet never seemed to touch the floor. Everything was unreal, dreamlike, moving in slow motion. Strange, blank faces bobbed at me from the pews, like rows of balloons on strings. Maria was still singing, but her voice sounded distant and discordant. My journey was endless. Reverend Brady was just a speck on the horizon; I feared he would not be reached before my trembling body gave out. The stale air tasted like paper as I sucked it in. I felt myself becoming uncertain as to exactly what it was I was trying to do. In the middle of that crowd I was completely alone. Something unfamiliar inside me whispered that I should sit down and think things over. After all, what was the hurry? A guy had the rest of his life to get saved.

To my dying day I will never know what might have happened if I had followed my own advice. But at my weakest moment a memory flashed before me which silenced the inner voice forever. I saw those turkeys sitting on the railroad tracks. I remembered how they had watched the train approaching, how they had heard the warning whistle, yet refused to move from the path of destruction. The analogy was clear: Tom Kane was one of those turkeys, and he was standing in Hell's way. Reverend Brady had just given a blast of the whistle to warn that danger was imminent. Sitting down and waiting would be fatal. I pushed onward and finally reached the front.

When all who wanted to come forward had done so, Reverend Brady asked us to bow our heads and repeat a simple prayer of salvation. We confessed our sins, asked Jesus to save us from them, and raised our faces to a glorious reality: we had just received the gift of eternal life. It was so easy, and yet the consequences were so far-reaching. All around me people hugged each other and wept. I shook so many hands, my palm cramped. Then someone was pulling on the back of my shirt.

"Guess what?" said Fred.

"What?"

"I did it too, Tommy. Now we'll always be together."

Fred might have been the only person on earth capable of dimming Heaven's glow. I could only hope that it was spacious enough up there to lose him now and then.

When it was finally possible to break loose of the crowd, I walked outside beneath the oak trees. A canopy of dark leaves obscured most of the stars, but a few were visible between the lower branches. The cooling night air was filled with the smell of hayfields and the sound of cars leaving the church. A soft breeze lifted my sweat-dampened hair. I sensed the presence of God around me, although if someone had asked me to explain how or why, I wouldn't have known what to say. A peace came over me that was beyond words. With the issue of eternity settled, the everyday problems now seemed so trivial. My inner turmoil was a sea of glass. The bottomless empty spot began to shrink and close as God's love washed over it.

I certainly didn't expect to cry, but tears came as suddenly as the flash of a shooting star. They seemed to be carrying the dissolved vestiges of hatred and bitterness that had festered inside me for so long. Each hot droplet, as it slid down my face, left me feeling lighter and cleaner. By the time I was ready to go back into the church, I felt like a new person. My sins were gone; the black hole was gone; my desire for revenge was gone. My family was also gone, and only a custodian remained to sweep the floors. I ran joyously back to the hotel to unveil the new Tom Kane.

• • • •

Reverend Brady's Volkswagen was parked in the driveway next to Grandpa's Chevy. Singing and laughter wafted out into the summer night as I opened the back door. In the kitchen Julia held a jug of apple cider in each hand, and Inez was shaking popcorn in a long-handled skillet.

"Thank goodness, Tommy," Julia said, pecking my cheek, "we were beginning to think you got lost. There's a little celebration going on in the dining room. Grab one of those glasses and join the fun."

"Tommy," said Inez, "before you leave, could I have you go to the parlor and see if Belle wants any popcorn? If she does, I'll have to set some aside before I add the butter. She's very picky about her weight, you know."

"Sure, but why is she in the parlor?"

"Who knows? When she was young, the children at school called her Dingdong Belle. At times I think they were quite accurate in their assessment."

I was still chuckling at my aunt's remark when I opened the parlor doors.

"What's your problem?" Belle asked sarcastically.

"I'm supposed to ask if you want any popcorn."

"Well, good for you. And now you can go tell whoever wants to know that your mission was completed. Thomas Kane did as he was told. Thomas Kane followed orders. Good, sweet, obedient Thomas Kane."

"Now what did I do?"

"Just what was expected, little fool. Nothing more, and certainly nothing less. The Chief expected you to be part of his sideshow, and I must say you performed admirably. Adorable little Thomas Kane marched right up front and got himself saved. I thought I was going to puke!"

"You were getting ready to do it too."

"Surely. But when I saw all the hypocrites jumping into the aisle, that old fool included, I changed my mind. I won't be part of a spectacle. I've got too much class for that."

Her indignation was so transparent that a thirteen-year-old could see through it.

"You're just mad because we took the spotlight off you. Anybody who got saved tonight was being honest about it. Going forward like that is too hard to do just to get yourself into somebody's will."

"Mr. Righteous," she scoffed.

"What about the popcorn?"

"Shove your popcorn."

I paraphrased her answer to Inez, then went to the dining room. Reverend Brady and Grandpa were singing "Sixteen Tons" to Maria's accompaniment. They were no threat to Tennessee Ernie Ford.

"Get over here and help us out," yelled the preacher when he saw me in the doorway.

"I'd rather just listen."

"Oh my," moaned Inez as she passed by, "I'd rather handle snakes than hear any more of that."

The unlikely duet ignored all insults and sang on. Dad motioned for me to come to him. He made room on the couch and offered the popcorn bowl that was balanced between his knees. For a while we were content to munch and endure the music. Then he spoke softly into my ear.

"Do you think I made a fool of myself tonight?"

"I think it was the smartest thing you've ever done."

He grinned, and I saw a hull on his tooth.

"Yeah, it was a good thing, but I bet you never figured your old man would pull something like that, did you."

"No way."

"Neither did your mother. I'm not sure she's too pleased."

"Why shouldn't she be?"

"Oh, I suspect she thinks I'm playing a game of some kind. She said the whole business made her uncomfortable."

Mom didn't look to be enjoying herself like the rest of us, and I could sympathize with the turmoil that was probably going on inside her heart. When one begins to wrestle with thoughts about God, the spirit seldom finds peace. I knew the agony of straddling the fence, wondering which way to jump. I was confident that she would make the right decision—and soon. After all, if Dad and I had seen the light, it must be shining very brightly.

The festivities continued another hour until the Bradys had to leave. Fred was sleeping on the couch by then, and Grandpa's voice was almost gone. We tried talking our guests into staying longer, but Maria said it was important that they get going. Tomorrow night their gospel crusade would continue in another place; there were still miles to go before they slept.

The preacher and his wife said their good-byes in the kitchen. Reverend Brady shook the hand of each family member, giving words of encouragement and that fabulous smile of his. I thought I had been inadvertently overlooked during the round of good-byes. But as he moved toward the back-porch door, Reverend Brady asked me to carry Maria's guitar to the car. The others remained inside as I followed the couple to the dew-covered Volkswagen. I was the slightest bit edgy because of my rude reaction to Maria hours before. I had wanted to apologize ever since returning to the hotel, but there were always people around her, and apologies were not easy.

"Just set that guitar in the back, Tom," said the preacher.

I pushed the seat ahead and carefully laid the instrument on top of a large travel bag. When I pulled my head back out of the car, both of them were right behind me, grinning.

"Tom Kane, I want you to meet my wife Maria. Sweetheart, this is my friend Tom Kane."

Maria laughed and took my hand. "I have this strange feeling that we've met before."

"That was another Tom Kane," said Reverend Brady. "You'll like this one a lot better."

"I'm sorry about . . . I just felt . . ."

"Don't worry about it," the preacher said. "We know all about what happened to your friend back in Iowa. Something like that is bound to mix a guy up. The important thing is not to let it ruin your whole life. You've learned a lot in the past few days, and you're a better man because of it. God will keep showing you His wisdom as long as you live; so be willing to accept it."

"Will you do me a favor, Tom?" Maria asked.

"Sure . . . what?"

"Forgive that man who killed your friend. I know that is a hard thing to do, but it needs to be done. I have forgiven you for something very small, and God has forgiven you for everything. If you can forgive that man for what he did, you will be free of all the pain that he put in your heart. Can you do it?"

"I think maybe I already have, back at the church."

Maria reached up and cupped my face in her hands.

"I'm glad I met you, Tom Kane. You are a very special young man."

"All Yankee fans are special, right, Tom?" said her husband.

"Right."

Two minutes later the Volkswagen vanished into the night. Reverend Brady's left hand waved to me as they faded into the darkness of Main Street. For a moment I felt despair setting in. Even though I had only known them a matter of hours, those two amazing people had impacted my world beyond description. Now they were gone. Would my new life begin to fade, like Cinderella's at the stroke of 12? Was this most beautiful of all bubbles about to burst?

I went back inside. The Chief was telling everyone good night.

"I want to stay up," he said, "but I can't remember when I've been so tired. I just hope I can make it to the bed."

"It's all the excitement these past two days, Poppa," said Julia. "But you don't have to worry about making it up the stairs."

She and Inez took him by the arms and prepared to ascend the red steps. I knew right then that the bubble was still there, shimmering and beautiful to the eye. I understood that the consequences of this night were not dependent upon the presence of the Bradys, but upon God. The preacher and his wife were only messengers carrying the good news of salvation and changed lives. Their job was finished. The miracles worked this night belonged to Jesus, and from this minute onward I would report directly to Him. As we all would. I knew this was true; the evidence was written on the joyous faces of those people standing next to me in the hotel.

As the aunts moved my great-grandfather toward the stairs, he whispered into Inez's ear. She stepped back, smiling and nodding her head. The Chief turned to Grandpa.

"Son, I'm afraid I've gotten to be too much of a burden for two frail women to handle. How about helping an old man up a mountain?"

Grandpa's chin quivered when he touched his father's arm. "I thought you'd never ask," he said.

The hall clock told us it was half past 10. It had been a long, long day. But the Chief's tired eyes were glistening as his children escorted him to his room. And so were ours.

IOWA

3

On Tuesday it was time to go home. Dad wanted to be on the road by 7, but it was closer to 8 when we gathered around the black Buick. Dark, heavy clouds hung low against the horizon. An occasional rumbling of thunder interrupted our good-byes.

"Junior, I don't think I'll be able to stand it after you've all gone," sniffled Julia. "We will be lost without someone to fuss over."

"We've gotten spoiled here, Julia," Dad said. "You and Inez took such good care of us that we won't know how to act when we get back home."

Inez handed Fred a sack of homemade fudge for the trip back.

"Remember now, Freddy, you must share with everybody, and don't eat too many of these because they are very rich."

"Fudges don't have money," he said, sticking his face into the sack.

The aunts tittered and played tug-of-war trying to give him a final squeeze. I was reminded of our arrival—when Fred had tried to do a cartwheel and hurt himself. They had fawned over him the same way. At that time they were just two old ladies in outdated dresses. Now they were precious pieces of my life, soon to be separated from me, and I was already feeling the pain of that separation.

"I'll write you both," I promised when they turned their attentions toward me.

"And we will hold you to that promise, young man," said Inez, blinking and wiping the corners of her eyes.

On the driver's side of the car, the Chief was talking to Dad and pointing a finger at him. I thought something was wrong, but then both of them laughed. They finally shook hands and turned quickly away, in the manner of men who are fighting to control their emotions.

Belle stood off to one side, arms folded, watching us struggle through the farewells. As I moved away from the aunts, she motioned me toward her. I was surprised; she hadn't said five words to me since Saturday night.

"Don't you feel just a little guilty, kiddo?"

"Why?"

"For heading back to civilization and leaving your poor, ancient cousin to dry-rot in this mausoleum."

"I'd trade places with you if I could," I said.

"Would you really?"

"Sure."

Belle looked me over from face to feet. She appeared tired. No longer did she remind me of a wicked queen; now she was just a middle-aged woman standing in front of a wilted lilac bush.

"Fly away home, little fool," she sighed, "before your coach turns into a pumpkin. I hope your dream world holds together, at least for a while."

I was left standing there as she turned and sauntered into the hotel, probably headed for the bathroom. Perhaps the mirror above the sink would tell her that she was the fairest of them all, but to me she was the saddest of them all. Like the rest of us, she had spent her years groping in darkness. Unlike us, when the light was finally revealed she rejected it and moved deeper into the shadows. The salvation message, which had melted colder hearts than her own, did not penetrate the hard shell of Cousin Belle. What would become of her in the years ahead?

The rest of my family was already in the car. The Chief handed me a round, metal can with a screw-down lid. It was heavy.

"I want you to have this as sort of a remembrance of your great-grandfather. He might not be around the next time you get down this way."

"You'll always be here, Chief, even when you're gone."

He gave me a touching smile.

"I think maybe there is a bit of the poet inside you, Thomas Jamison, and much more than that too. I want to say that I respect you for the way you stood up to me the other night. You had a part in helping me find out how wrong I had been, and I'm grateful. You are a credit to the name of Kane, and I'm proud to be of the same blood. Take care, son."

We shook hands; he held mine a long time.

"Let's ride, Tom," Dad said softly.

The Chief stepped back as I closed the car door. Fred was cramming fudge into his mouth, dropping crumbs onto his pants. The backseat already had a layer of comic books covering it. I cleared away enough of them to sit down, then removed the lid from the can to see what the Chief had given me. It was half-full of Indianhead pennies.

"I saved them over the years," he said through the window as the car backed slowly toward the street.

"I don't deserve something like this," I protested.

"You don't deserve broken glass either," he called after me.

Julia and Inez were waving as Dad shifted the transmission from reverse to drive. The Chief waved too. How had he known?

Dad honked the horn as we turned left onto Main Street. I watched the hotel grow small through the back window.

"What was that business about broken glass?" Dad asked after Climer had become part of the car's dust cloud.

"Oh, it's a long story."

"One of those kind that sounds better after a little time goes by, I suppose."

"That's exactly the kind it is."

Dad nodded. "I've been there once or twice."

"Where?" asked Fred, straining to see whatever might be up ahead.

My father looked over his shoulder and laughed. "Give me some of that fudge, you little hog."

• • • •

Grandpa was waiting for us outside the gas station. He wore some sort of blue work uniform and a St. Louis Cardinals baseball cap.

"Fill 'er up?"

"Sure," said Dad, making an exaggerated study of Grandpa's clothes, "but what's the deal with these?"

"Style, Junior. I decided if I'm gonna run a station, then I better get out here an' start doin' it. There was lotsa times I wouldn't even come outside to wait on customers if I'd been hittin' the sauce. Now I feel like sweatin' a little an' gettin' some grease on my fingers again. Let ol' Ruthie pour the beer, an' I'll pump the gas. Who knows, we might get rich an' quit speakin' to the common folks. Wouldn't that be a kick?"

"It sure would, Dad."

Grandpa took a piece of fudge and admired my pennies while the pump ran.

"Them was the only kind of pennies they had when I was a kid. Indian pennies, Indian nickels, Indians everyplace. Maybe that's how I got that little bald patch on the back of my head."

He looked good. His eyes were bright and clear; there was a spark of vitality that hadn't been evident before. My grandfather truly resembled a man born again.

"What is that, about three-seventy?" asked Dad, checking the price on the pump.

"No charge for people in black Buicks."

Dad pulled out his billfold. "C'mon now, let's not have any of that."

"You know what, Junior? It's been more than twenty years since I put you over my knee, but that don't mean I still can't get it done."

"Do it, do it," begged Fred.

"That would be interesting," Mom admitted. "I've wished I could beat him myself at least ten thousand times."

Realizing he was outnumbered, Dad gave in and accepted the free gas. There were other gifts as well, including sacks of fireworks for me and Fred.

"Those things are illegal in Iowa," Dad warned Grandpa.

"Illegal! What kind of place you livin' in up there? Don't they know explodin' crackers is a way of life, for cryin' out loud?"

"We'll use them anyway," I said.

"Attaboy, Tommy. Just cuz we're goin' to Heaven now don't

mean we can't have a little fun once in a while." He turned to Mom. "C'mere, Louise, I got something for you that every girl in Sedalia used to dream about."

He proceeded to give her a bent-over-backwards kiss. Mom blushed like a teenager. Fred and I laughed until our sides cramped.

We stalled as long as possible, but finally Dad said it was time to hit the road. One by one we hugged Grandpa and told him how much we would miss him. I noticed, while holding him close, that he didn't smell of whiskey. The earliness of the hour might have accounted for that, but I hoped it was a sign he had quit drinking. What would that small miracle be to a God who had just saved his soul?

When we were back inside the car, Dad snapped his fingers, got out again, and trotted inside the station. Grandpa watched him, appearing to be as uncertain as we were. Gigantic raindrops began smacking the windshield while we waited. In less than a minute Dad was back outside giving his father one last embrace and then hurrying to the car.

"Get a dry shirt on," he yelled to Grandpa as we drove past him.

"Keep your eyes on the road, ya knucklehead," Grandpa called back.

Rain pounded the Buick as we pulled onto the blacktop. It seemed we were driving into the streams of a dozen firehoses. The wipers had a minimal effect, forcing Dad to drive with his nose next to the windshield.

Ten minutes later, when the precipitation ended, it was as if the clouds had totally exhausted themselves. Almost immediately patches of blue appeared. A perfect rainbow arced across the brightening sky. We watched in silent awe until the crescent of color faded.

"Why did you go into the station?" Mom asked Dad.

"I wanted to tell someone good-bye."

"I thought nobody was in there but Ruth."

"That's right."

Mom looked at him and shook her head in disbelief. "I'm going to sleep so I can wake up and prove this was just a dream."

I caught Dad's eye in the rearview mirror. He winked. We were five hundred miles from home.

• • • •

Mom and Fred had been sleeping a long time when Dad drove the Buick into a gas station with a green dinosaur on the sign. When the pimple-faced attendant came out, I knew this was the same place we had stopped at on the way down.

"What kin ah do fer you-all today?" If he recognized us, it didn't show.

"Fill it with regular," Dad said, "and check the oil."

Mom opened her eyes and stared sleepily at the restroom sign.

"Tommy, wake your brother and take him to the toilet while we're stopped."

When he was tired or sick, Fred had a tendency to overestimate the capacity of his bladder. A spotted mattress back home was testimony to that fact. It took several minutes for me to maneuver him to the restroom and back again. The attendant was just slamming the hood as we got into the car.

"Oil looks good, sir. The gas'll be three dollars 'n' fourteen cents."

Dad handed him a twenty and started the engine. The guy fumbled through his pockets for change. We started moving.

"Keep it," Dad said.

Mom's eyes were huge, but the pimple-faced kid looked like his were about to pop.

"All of it? Yuh mean keep all of it? This here's a twenty-dollar bill, mister. Hey, thanks a bunch!"

Dad squealed the tires across the hot pavement leading home.

"Oh boy, Dad's peeling out," Fred said.

"You get back to sleep," snapped Mom.

Fred started to protest, but the mention of sleep triggered an automatic response. His eyes fluttered. Within a minute he had burrowed into the junk on the seat, making soft grunting sounds like a pig searching for the perfect spot in a slophole.

"What was the point of that ridiculous tip?" demanded Mom.

"Didn't you remember that place?" asked Dad.

"It's just a gas station."

"Not quite. That guy back there was the same one who gave us too much money when we stopped here before. Remember how mad you got when I wouldn't turn around? Well, now he's got it all back."

At first Mom was speechless. Twice she tried saying something, but succeeded only in forming empty words with her lips. "Johnathon Kane," she finally muttered, "I'm beginning to think you're not the same man who drove us down here."

"He's not," I said.

Dad only grinned, keeping his eyes on the road. He had come a long way in a short time, and not just from Climer, Missouri.

• • • •

The sun had set by the time we reached home, but twilight allowed us to unload the car without breaking our necks. What an odd feeling it was to return and find everything so uninviting. McKinley looked dirty and ugly. After experiencing Climer's rural serenity, the noise and commotion of our town were unpleasant distractions. The house itself was a sorry sight compared to the grandeur of the hotel. Dropping suitcases on the living room floor, I realized that our furniture wouldn't have been fit for the attic in Missouri. The contrast was disheartening. Instead of cut glass and fuzzy wallpaper, we had cut linoleum and fuzzy waterpipes. Rather than paintings upon the walls, we had calendars picturing speckled trout or the local office of some insurance agency.

To make things worse, after two weeks of being closed up, the house smelled like a mountain of Fred's socks. It didn't help any that a mouse had been executed in a trap sometime during our absence. I found the whole business of coming home extremely depressing. Mom didn't share my feelings.

"Isn't it nice to be back in our own house again, Tommy," she sighed, flopping down on a worn-out blue sofa with sagging arms.

"I s'pose."

Dad laid the last bag of dirty clothes on top of the suitcases and slumped to the floor.

"Kind of hard to get back in the old groove, isn't it, son?"

"Uh huh."

"Well, it will be for me too. I'm not looking forward to going back to the plant, but I've got to. That's the way it is. A lot of things have happened to us lately, and we'll just have to sort them out as we go along."

"Hippo's outside," Fred yelled through the screen.

As I walked past Dad to the door, he pulled me aside and spoke low so Mom wouldn't hear.

"Remember, you're all finished with that Mexican business."

"No problem."

"What were you two whispering about?" Mom asked as I pushed open the screen.

"We were discussing your birthday present," Dad said.

"My birthday isn't for three months."

"No sense waiting until the last minute, is there?"

Mom threw her shoe at him.

Hippo was wearing his same sweaty clothes and a familiar grin. He sat in the porch swing as if nothing had changed, as if two weeks hadn't passed, as if my whole life wasn't forever altered by events happening since I left McKinley. Hippo Reeves, the friend of my youth, sat in that swing like it was just another Summer evening. To him, I guess maybe it was.

"Hiya, Tommy."

"Hello, Hippo."

"Hey, you was gone a long time, man. I thought maybe you ran out on us for good."

"Two weeks."

"Well, you shoulda been here because things really got hot."

"What things?"

Even in the fading light I could see his eyes bug.

"What things do you think? That Mexican—Carlos Montez—and his family."

"Oh."

"Yeah, from what I hear, the guy who owns the Mexican shack has threatened to kick that big mama out if she don't get the paint off the walls. You never did see what it looked like in the daytime, Tommy. We did a job on it, I'll say that much. It would take a month to get all that off, and as soon as she does we'll do it again. Hey, did you know Montez's trial starts in a week?"

"Yeah? Well, I don't care too much about Carlos Montez anymore."

Hippo's head spun around. "What's that mean?"

"I mean whatever happened, happened. And we won't bring Jimmy back by keeping things stirred up. Carlos Montez will get what's coming to him without any help from us."

"Are you nuts? Jimmy was our friend, an' you're the one who thought paintin' that shack was such a great idea in the first place. I think something must have happened to you while you were gone."

"You're right, Hippo . . . Something did happen. Just like what happened to Jimmy when he was at camp."

"What's that?"

"I got saved."

My friend gave me the same blank look he had once given our reading teacher when she asked him for the names of the two young lovers in *Romeo and Juliet*.

"Saved?"

"That's what I said. S-a-v-e-d, saved."

"I don't get it."

"Look, Hippo, I'm talking about something that isn't explained in thirty seconds. It took a long time for the whole thing to sink into my thick skull, and you won't be any different. All I want to say about it now is that I don't think the same way about things as I used to. I've changed some, and I know now that what we did to them Mexicans wasn't right. Tomorrow I might even walk over there and tell the woman I did it. Maybe I can help clean some of it up."

"You're crazy," Hippo yelled. "We could get in big trouble over that deal. We took a vow of silence. I sure never figured you'd stab me in the back like that, Kane."

"Did I say one word about mentioning anyone else? You can do whatever you like, but I'm through playing stupid war games. I'll confess to my part of it, and nobody ever has to know the rest. But if you want to come with me tomorrow, it would be a lot easier."

"No chance, baby. We did a good thing, an' now you want to mess it up."

"It wasn't a good thing, Hippo. It just seemed like it at the time."

"Is that a fact? Well, I didn't get 'saved' or whatever that was, so it still looks good to me. And if you're smart, you'll go back to the way you used to be or maybe I'll have to pound your face!"

I couldn't help laughing.

"Hippo, if you knew all the people I've been nose to nose with the past two weeks, you wouldn't bother me with such puny threats. How about coming along tomorrow?"

My friend stood up and walked across the porch to his bike.

"If you go to the Mexican place tomorrow or any other time, you'll walk alone and I'll hate your guts for a million years!"

With that said, he mounted the bike and rode into the night. I considered running after him, but decided it might be better to let his anger cool until morning. Maybe by then he would be more receptive to what I had to say.

I sat in the swing a while longer as a full moon floated higher in the black sky. Nearby a mournful owl asked the question that owls have been asking since creation. The distant sounds of squealing brakes and rumbling mufflers signaled the onset of McKinley's nightlife. Inside the house, my parents were opening windows and beginning the long process of getting things back to normal.

I knew that in a day or two the transition from Missouri to McKinley—from hotel to hovel—would be completed. Life would resume familiar patterns: the heat, the boredom, the frustrations of day-to-day living in a lower-income family. Only one thing had actually changed, but what a difference it made. Despite what Hippo had just said, Tom Kane would never again walk alone!

· · · ·

Hippo overestimated how long he would hate me by a million years minus one week. The day I went to the Mexican house to confess, he followed at a distance, taunting me with obscene names and gestures. Ignoring him was fairly simple; the closer we got to the scene of our crime, the farther back he lagged. By the time I reached my destination, he was a small, silent dot on the horizon.

The Mexican woman had trouble understanding what I was trying to tell her.

"I'm the one who messed up your house."

"Messy house?"

"Me—I did it—I painted your house a couple weeks ago."

"Couple weeks? Messy house?"

She pointed to clothes strewn across the furniture and floor, a perplexed look on her face. We might never have bridged the communication gap had it not been for the boy. He emerged from a back room and listened wide-eyed to what I was saying. A few hundred syllables of Spanish were relayed to the mother. Finally comprehending, the woman turned back to me, hands on hips, and fired off some words of her own. They didn't sound complimentary. But when the boy explained that I would attempt to undo the damage, she softened her tone considerably. By the time I left, she was patting me on the shoulder and saying, "Nice man, good nice man."

Hippo met me at the tracks.

"Did ya tell?" he asked, smacking a fist into a palm.

"I told my part of it."

"What about mine?"

"Your name never came up."

He spit on the ground. "You might be lyin'."

"Yeah, and you might be close to eating your teeth."

I doubt that Reverend Brady would have approved of how I handled the situation, but it couldn't be helped. Eventually, after much verbal sparring, we went a few rounds. Hippo might have gotten the best of me, but not enough to make up for the split lip and bloody nose he received. That fight pretty much ended the whole business, except for several days of the silent treatment. After that, we made up; our friendship would endure and grow even stronger.

As I sat in the porch swing that evening, staring out at the street, I noticed that the dark spot left by Jimmy's blood had completely disappeared. How fitting. It seemed as if the spot had merely been a reflection of the darkness lurking inside my own heart. As the powerful saving love of Christ had removed the stain of sin and hatred from within me, likewise the spot in the street had faded into nothingness. There was no longer any reason for despair, no reason for tears. With the shadows of dusk lengthening around me, and with fireflies winking at each other above the front lawn, I was at peace with the memory of Jimmy Swailes. He was safe and in loving arms. Though separated from him temporarily, I knew we would meet again someday in a place more wonderful than words could tell. As Maria Brady promised in song, inside a little white church with a spired steeple, when the roll is called up yonder, we'll be there!